A Child's War

Memories of a child in London during World War II

David L. Gordon

© 2008 David L. Gordon. All rights reserved.
ISBN 978-0-578-00433-4

DEDICATION

To the memory of my dear parents, who like countless other Londoners lost their home, health and everything they had worked for due to the tragedy of World War II. To my patient wife Barbara, who has tirelessly encouraged me to record this story of my childhood. Finally, to my son Edward without whom 'A Child's War' would never have been completed.

CONTENTS

Dedication	3
Contents	4
Evacuated from Parents to an Unknown Destination	5
Food Rationing – Survivors of Dunkirk Return	16
The Bloody "Froggies" Have Capitulated	29
London "Blitz". Luftwaffe Bombs Day and Night	41
A New School – Sadistic Teachers	54
Hess defects – Dog Fights	67
Our Parents Visit – America Comes to Our Aid	79
Home Guard – Sex Was Taboo	92
The Yanks Arrive – Tootsie Rolls & Chewing Gum	104
Attacked by a G.I. – Barrack Room Fights	116
D-Day Arrives – A Quick Get-Away	128
Italian Prisoners of War	141
Flying Bombs and V2 Rockets Land on London	153
Finally Home – World War II Is Over	169
Appendix	177

Evacuated from Parents to an Unknown Destination

"Once again we must fight for life and honour against all the might and fury of the valiant, disciplined and ruthless German race."
Sir Winston Churchill

As soon as I woke up I knew something was going to happen, but for a moment I couldn't think what it was. I looked across to my little brother, still asleep in the next bed and over to the window-seat where two small suitcases packed with neatly folded clothes suddenly reminded me. My stomach gave a lurch. Today we were going to be evacuated! I got out of bed and went over to John. I shook him lightly and he opened his eyes.
"Come on, we must get up – we're going away today remember?"
His eyes clouded over.
"Don't want to go away."
"Well, you don't want to stay here and get bombed, do you?" Of course the words were virtually meaningless to him as he was only four years old. I, at eight, was at an age when anything new or out of the usual run of things, was an adventure.
It was late August 1939, and apparently there was going to be a war. Fear that this would eventually happen had been growing for a long time and the London County Council had laid plans for the evacuation of thousands of children from their London homes to the comparative safety of the country. Instructions had been given

to parents advising them to prepare the bare necessities together with sufficient food for the journey. Each child was allowed only one small suitcase.

We dressed carefully and went down to breakfast. Mother had cooked our favourite - two eggs, fried on both sides sitting on two pieces of crisp fried bread. We ate with gusto but Mother and Father only drank coffee I remember. I had been conscious that my parents were very quiet and serious lately and several times I had caught my mother looking at us with such an expression of sadness on her face that I had gone up to her and putting my arms around her waist had buried my face in her apron without knowing what moved me to such a demonstration of affection - although in those early days I was a very uncomplicated and extrovert child.

The first hint that something serious was happening had been brought home to me when my brother and I were at the Saturday morning cinema show the week before. These sessions which started at 9 a.m. were the highlight of our week. The films were mostly cartoon serials - Flash Gordon; Jungle Jim and others I've forgotten. Sometimes 'real' film stars would make personal appearances, and sometimes there were talent competitions where prizes were given to the fortunate winners. The entrance fee for this wealth of delight was three-pence! On this last visit, we had seen the newsreel showing the Prime Minister Neville Chamberlain returning from his talks with Adolf Hitler bringing assurance that there would be no war! Now suddenly everything was changed - our world was turned upside down and we were leaving home.

After breakfast we finished packing - putting in our toothbrushes and face flannels and the few small favourite toys we were taking. We each had a suitcase; a packet of food and a small bottle of lemonade, and of course, our gas-masks in their square cardboard boxes which we slung over our shoulders by the attached cord.

We set off from our London home quite early for although Waterloo Station was not far away we had been warned that travelling conditions would be chaotic - so many children going to so many different places. To add to the bewilderment, one of the most distressing aspects was the fact that no one knew where they were going. We were being sent in 'School-loads' and only the headmaster or mistress of each school had the address – in a sealed envelope.

On arrival at the station, there was a seething mass of children, each one tagged with his or her own name and the name of the school which it attended. With their labels fastened to their lapels by a length of string they resembled pieces of baggage waiting to be shipped to some foreign port!

It was all overwhelming and I clutched my mother's hand tight - I was afraid I would get swept away in the crowd and be lost forever.

We didn't know where to go. My parents had been told that the name of each school would be well displayed and we should assemble at the appropriate place, but there were so many cardboard placards, a large number of them indecipherable that it would have taken all day to push our way through to examine each one! Suddenly by sheer luck we saw a hand-written sign with the name of my school on it. We made our way over to the large group among which I recognised the familiar faces of my school friends. I was soon chatting excitedly but John, of course, had not started school yet and had no friends to talk to. His little white face peered out from the shelter of my father's arms for he had been picked up for safety while we pushed through the crowds.

After a long wait my teacher approached my parents.

"I think you should say goodbye now, we shall be boarding the train soon." She moved on to the family standing behind us and repeated the suggestion. I felt stunned - I still couldn't believe that we were going away and didn't know when we would be back. John began to cry as my father put him down, automatically I took his hand. Our parents bent and kissed us, my mother had tears in her eyes and she hugged me very hard. Then they were gone and we were alone.

The assumption that we were about to board the train was misfounded. We stood in a tight group for almost another hour. The noise of trains shunting to and fro and the shouting of the over-worked teachers and station staff trying to get the children sorted out was like a bad dream.

At last we moved up to the barrier of a platform and slowly made our way through to where a large black engine, steam belching from its funnel, was waiting to pull a long line of carriages full of unhappy children away from their homes to an unknown destination somewhere in the country.

We were herded in - ten to each compartment built to hold six and then once more we waited. Although it was only the end of August it was an autumn-like day and as we waited a fog descended. We were all very hungry and we opened our packets of food and ate ravenously - later we were to regret our recklessness.

With a powerful whistle the engine started to move and we were off! At first it was interesting to look out of the windows, especially as we began to leave London and its suburbs behind and get into open country. I was a London child, bred and born, and had not been into 'the country' more than half a dozen times. But soon the fog became denser and it was difficult to see anything clearly and I became bored.

Because of the overcrowding we were very uncomfortable and soon we all got very irritable. Occasionally someone would start to cry until 'hushed' crossly by his or her companions and gradually we fell into an uneasy silence.

We kept stopping and starting and every so often we were shunted into a siding for what seemed hours before with a shriek and puffing of steam the engine would set off again. Gradually one by one we fell asleep but it was only 'cat-napping' and was not very restful. By mid-evening we were all extremely hungry but because of our previous improvidence we had no food left.

I don't know how long it was before we stopped with a shudder for what was to be the last time, waking us all - we had arrived at our destination! Voices could be heard outside in the night - strange voices shouted, as with a bang the doors were flung open and we were told to gather our belongings and get off the train. We had no idea where we were but later I learned it had taken fourteen hours to travel one hundred and twenty miles.

We were at a dimly-lit railway station somewhere in the south of England.

The voices of the officials talking amongst themselves were strange - almost foreign, monotone voices sounding like the buzzing at a bumble bee in a jug. They herded us along the platform - like cattle, going to the slaughter - or that's how it felt to us.

We were taken to the waiting room where we were to be handed over to our foster parents who had volunteered to look after one or more children in their homes. They had answered a government call to take in evacuees from the cities, for which they were paid a few shillings a week to cover the cost of food and keep. Some were parents with children of their own, others were childless. With a few exceptions all were eager to assist in some way this national crisis - others no doubt, saw an opportunity of financial gain.

There, blinking in the dim light, cold, hungry, sleepy and miserable, and hardly taking in anything of the scene except the crowd of strangers waiting for us, my brother and I and several others were 'claimed' by a large, untidy, red-faced woman and a thin dark-haired, dejected looking little man who turned out to be -

naturally enough - her husband. We were hurried out of the station and along a dark road outside. Stumbling along silently with sleep-bleared eyes we couldn't judge how far it was nor what type of neighbourhood we had come to and we were past caring. I hardly noticed the house where at last our journey ended. We stumbled up some stairs and fell into bed to sleep the clock round.

Sometime during the next day I awoke in the house which was to be my home for the next few weeks. Still dazed from the experience of the past twenty-four hours, I looked around the room where I had slept. It was quite a large room but contained no furniture other than two beds. One (the smaller) occupied by my brother and me, the other by four children who were now peering at us suspiciously from under a large flowered eiderdown. We had been roused at last by the appearance of our foster mother who spoke with a deep and very loud voice in a strong Cockney accent. "Well, well, so yer awake at last! Wot a sorry sight yer all was last night. Well, come on - rise and shine, I can't 'ave my morning's work upset anymore!"

Her chequered apron covered an enormous stomach and was stained with all manner of food and dirt, and this she was to wear continuously for the duration of our stay. On her head she wore a black hairnet which covered her unkempt greasy hair. This was Mrs Barton.

The next few weeks were weeks of living in incredible filth: Beds to sleep in with blankets which had not been washed for years, and cold water to wash in each morning. The light in most rooms consisted of a solitary light bulb dangling from the centre of the ceiling, accompanied by a hanging fly-paper dotted with dead flies, and what carpets and rugs there were on the floors were threadbare.

Saturday night by Mrs Barton's rules was bath night and that first Saturday was a memorable occasion. We were all sent up to the bedroom at six o'clock and told to undress completely. Two of our number were girls aged eight and nine respectively (they slept with their two younger brothers in the other bed) and although coming from a mixed family, the depth of embarrassment and degradation they were reduced to, at having to comply with this ruling, was pitiful. Naked and shivering we lined up outside the bathroom door. My brother John, being the youngest was the first in the tub. He submitted docilely enough to the callous scrubbing administered by our benefactress, then as she turned away to get the towel with a rough command: "Out yer get then - look lively," he automatically leaned forward and pulled out the plug. Mrs Barton rounded on him like a positive virago.

"Wot the 'ell d'yer think yer doing, yer little bleeder? Wot ter abaht the uvvers then?" I can remember her words to this day for the scene is etched indelibly on my memory. In the corner of the bathroom was a large copper pot used for boiling water for the weekly bath and for boiling the washing in. A copper stick, bleached white and used to remove scalding washing was within easy reach. Grabbing the stick she began to beat my brother unmercifully in front of the terrified audience of children watching fearfully from the doorway, whacking his back, legs and backside and paying no attention to his cries as he screamed repeatedly: "I didn't know! I didn't know!"

I am not very proud of my reaction - I was petrified. Afterwards I railed myself for not springing to John's defence but at the time I could only watch as his little body became covered with scarlet weals, terrified in case this brutality was going to be inflicted on me as well. However the rest of us were spared bodily harm other than that inflicted by having to bathe in icy cold water and dry on a thin skimpy towel that by the time the last of us used it was completely saturated.

Life settled into a dreary routine. Meals were served in the scullery, on a large wooden table which was big enough for all of us to sit round. Here we would sit for breakfast before going to school. Our cocoa was made with water and was served with two slices of bread and 'marg' - bread and jam on more fortunate occasions (I believe on Sunday mornings only).

We walked to school each morning and back again in the late afternoon having been given milk at morning break and lunch at noon.

Because of the sudden influx of pupils to the little town, the schools were hopelessly overcrowded and during this time our lessons were very disjointed and to me very boring. I had enjoyed school in London and had felt a desire to excel. The competitive spirit had been encouraged and I had begun to develop quite a lively interest in the world around me. Here in the country life was lived at a much slower pace and I found I could get by with the minimum amount of work.

One day as I was walking back through the chestnut-lined streets I was conscious of a terrible itching on my head. I scratched it hard but a few minutes later it was irritating worse than ever. When I got home I was still scratching. Mrs Barton's-sharp eyes raked over me.

"Wot's s up with you then?"

"My head itches badly."

"Come 'ere."

I went over to where she was stirring a thick grey greasy stew in an iron pot on the kitchen range. She pulled my head down and started running her dirty fingers through my hair. Suddenly several little black insects fell from my head onto the floor - one even disappeared into the pot.

"You've got lice." The words were said with a certain venomous satisfaction. "I'll deal with you ternight, my lad."

During the evening each one of us was scrutinised and it was discovered that five out of the six of us were 'lousy'.

Before supper - during which, incidentally, I tried not to think of the lice which had dropped in the stew - Mrs Barton systematically 'de-loused' us. First our hair was cut to within an inch of our heads by an enormous pair of scissors. We boys were not too concerned, but the girls wept bitterly as their locks fell in pathetic heaps onto the floor. Then we had to immerse our heads in a sink full of water liberally laced with disinfectant. Finally Mrs Barton rubbed vast quantities of vinegar all over our scalps.

It was drastic treatment but we were never troubled again by our 'little visitors'!

By now the authorities were getting the various problems sorted out after the confusion caused by the arrival of the evacuees. Officials were systematically visiting the homes to see what type of conditions and what type of persons were taking in these 'war-orphans'.

One of these inspectors arrived at Mrs Barton's 'Baby Farm'. We were at school so I do not know what transpired. All I know is that when we came in at five o'clock there was a car outside the door and a strange man was loading our meagre belongings in the boot. Mrs Barton was in the kitchen looking very dejected. The same black hairnet on her greasy hair and the same dirty chequered apron covering her fat belly. No doubt, as we were whisked away from her not-so-tender care, she was puzzling over why the authorities had deprived her of the chance to help the nation during this emergency!

FOOD RATIONING – SURVIVORS OF DUNKIRK RETURN

"The transition from peace to war has been accomplished."
Sir Winston Churchill, December 12, 1939.

After the horrible experiences of the last few weeks, special care bad been taken to place us with a suitable family and a couple had been found who were prepared to take my brother and me into their home. We did not know it at the time, but we were to stay with Mr and Mrs Carpenter for the duration of the war as their adopted children - although at no time during our stay did I ever consider them my adopted parents!

Mr and Mrs Carpenter lived on the outskirts of the town in a row of council houses which was in fact, the last row before the country widened out into arable farmland. The houses looked identical except for the colour of the front door. Each one had a small garden in front and a larger area of ground at the back which in every case was used for the growing of vegetables to help the war effort. The Government was at this time urging the population to produce as much as possible and 'Dig for Victory' posters adorned several trees and walls in the towns as well as such places as railway station waiting-rooms.

Our first day at our new home was a very pleasant change. The traditional Sunday lunch of roast beef and potatoes baked around the meat was the best meal we had had for weeks. Served with fresh country vegetables and followed by a steam pudding covered with treacle, it was the most delicious lunch any young boy could have wished for – we were even allowed 'seconds' of the pudding. In the evening we were both given a hot bath, then off to bed in a room to ourselves with a huge double bed so high from the ground that we literally had to climb into it! The linen smelled clean and fresh and for the first time since we had left home we really relaxed.

Inevitable we were lonelier in our new home and missed pals. Although Mrs Barton had treated us to the minimal amount of care and attention, the very fact of shared hardship had made us a close-knit band and we wondered what had happened to them and where they had been sent.

John settled down better than I. Mr and Mrs Carpenter had no children of their own and I suppose my brother's tender age awoke their protective instincts. I could never get used to the discipline which to me seemed so suppressive that as time went by I took every chance to stay away and only returned 'home' to eat and sleep.

The house was small but compact and spotlessly clean and tidy. Mrs Carpenter was an extremely competent housewife. She took great pride in varying our diet as much as possible and I never heard her grumble about the difficulty of providing meals with such meagre rations. Admittedly it consisted mainly of good country vegetables like parsnips and cabbage. It was almost a meatless diet. Once or twice a week we ate fish-cakes which were ninety per cent potatoes and the rest cod or, once in a while sausages which were mainly bread.

People in the suburban towns generally fared better than those in the cities. Little gastronomical luxuries like pheasants, hares or grouse could be found but, unlike many European countries where horse is considered a luxury, even in this time of shortage the British never overcame their distaste for it and I don't think I ever heard of it being eaten.

Whale meat was sometimes offered by the butcher; this was anaemic looking meat with a very definite flavour of oil. Within each family a certain amount of bartering went on, exchanging items of food which you disliked for something you preferred. For years I do not recall tasting a piece of cheese; Mr Carpenter would eat the entire cheese ration for the household. But to compensate, as children, we would get his weekly ration of sweets. The butter ration of two ounces a week was mixed with margarine to make it go further. Four ounces of sugar was never enough even if one gave up sweetened tea and coffee in order to save it for cooking. For the whole of the war I never saw an orange or lemon, they just were not imported. The only foreign 'fruit' we ever tasted was dehydrated bananas! A greyish yellow powder that when mixed with water resembled in taste and texture mashed bananas - these were usually only obtainable from food parcels from America and were few and far between.

The most comfortable room in the house was the kitchen, where the winter chill had been taken off by the steam from the cooking.

This is where we ate most meals, at the scullery table. In the evenings the coal fire was lit in the sitting room, around which we sat as near as possible to get warm, our faces burning from the heat of the coals and our backs unpleasantly cold. Bedtime was an ordeal where, in an unheated room, the temperature was sometimes so cold that you could see your own breath. It took great effort, like jumping into an icy pool, to get into bed, the sheets sometimes so cold that they felt almost damp, it was wise to keep both socks and underwear on until the bed was warm enough to discard them. In a very short time we had settled down completely in our new home, it was as if we had lived there for months. We liked our 'parents' quite well although they were very strict with us and very precise in everything they did. Meal-times were inflexible, served absolutely on the dot. If we were late - we got no food. Similarly bedtime never varied - six o'clock for John, seven forty-five for me.

We still attended the same school (which was a London school transferred with all the teachers to the country) but now we had farther to walk. There were no buses available and it was nearly three miles each way. However we used to pick up friends on the way and by the time we arrived we were quite a collection.

At school we all helped to dig trenches which were within easy reach of the classrooms, and practised evacuating to them in preparation for an air attack by the Germans. We rehearsed daily the routine of clearing the classrooms and getting into the trenches, face down, in three minutes flat, the signal being given by the teacher by a blast on a whistle - sometimes in the middle of a lesson.

In class we were often made to sit wearing our gas-masks for long periods. These practice sessions were most unpleasant as it was extremely difficult to breathe naturally while wearing the mask. It was possible, if undetected by the teacher, to slip one's chin out. This made breathing much easier, but rather defeated the object of the lesson.

We were also told how to protect ourselves in the event of an air attack by lying under the school desks, face down with our arms covering our heads.

By now, clothing as well as food was rationed. Clothing coupons were issued, together with a chart which showed how many coupons were required for each item. For most people the allocation was sufficient for them to be respectably dressed, but the selection in the shops was very limited.

Similarly the food was sufficient so that we did not go hungry, but at the same time, as youngsters, we could never get enough to eat! Every effort was made to see we got our school milk, which we could buy at every mid-morning and mid-afternoon break. This was not free, but cost a halfpenny for a small bottle.

Sometimes it was possible to get a bag of stale cakes from the baker's – cakes which had not been sold and were anything between one and three days old. Occasionally we would find a fresh one in the bag of cakes for which we would pay the baker one penny. Some cold evenings, on the long walk home from school, we would stop and buy a fresh loaf of bread to eat, using the money which had been intended for our school milk. This bread was often straight from the baker's oven and was so deliciously hot that it would burn our fingers as we pulled off chunks of the soft dough.

A routine became established, broken only by visits to the cinema or occasionally to the homes of friends in the enviable position of being billeted on foster parents with large families of their own and to whom a few more 'kids around the place' made little difference. The chief difficulty when socializing was the meagre hospitality one could provide for one's friends because of the rationing. A ration book for food was issued to everyone but the weekly ration was revised from month to month depending on the availability of supplies. The blockade of Britain had begun and few ships could be spared to bring foodstuffs from abroad - many were sunk by the enemy before reaching our shores.

At this time we were only vaguely aware of the progress of the War, but in fact in 1940, things were not going well for the Allies. It was generally understood that Hitler had a plan for the invasion of France involving Belgium and Holland and that a section of the British Army known the B.E.F. (British Expeditionary Force) was planning and training for the day when they would be shipped across the channel to join the French Army which according to Winston Churchill did not view the war "with uprising spirit or even much confidence. The restless internal politics of the past decade had bred disunity and discontents . The long winter months of waiting gave time and opportunity for the poisons to be established" (The Gathering Storm).

Early in March the Germans attacked shipping along the East Coast and in April Hitler invaded and occupied Norway. Bitter fighting in Norwegian waters did however result in the virtual destruction of the German Navy (by the end of June it consisted of one eight-inch cruiser, two light cruisers and four destroyers!) During the first two weeks of May 1940, the Germans launched a strong attack on the French Line and on the 14th broke through near Sedan. Britain was sending as much support as she could spare, but it was imperative not to leave herself undefended for if the Germans captured France – which as the weeks went by seemed a distinct possibility – it was but a short hop across the Channel to invade England.

The breakthrough at Sedan was followed by nearly a dozen motorised German Divisions pushing home their advantage and the French had not enough reserve forces to stem the surge. Where the line was broken became known as "The Bulge". Britain increased her aid with more troops and more Air Force Squadrons but the Germans pushed relentlessly on, their 'Chars Allemandes" – powerful tanks – crushing all before them on their unimpeded way.

On May 20th, the enemy entered Abbeville and by so doing successfully ended a manoeuvre to cut off the communications of the whole Northern Armies. The British and French troops were forced nearer and nearer to the sea.

The Admiralty now put into operation a plan to assemble "a large number of small vessels in readiness to proceed to ports and inlets on the French coast" (Minutes of a meeting of the War Cabinet, May 20th, 1940).

The situation worsened and on May 27th the B.E.F. was withdrawn, and the evacuation of Dunkirk began.

By now, the town of Dunkirk was in flames and the defeated British and French armies were pressed into a small area on the waterfront. Hitler's Airforce, artillery and what was left of the Navy, were given orders to destroy what remained of the allied forces on the beaches and in the water.

British and French naval vessels evacuated men waiting in their thousands, many of them trying to keep afloat in the water, wounded, exhausted, bewildered, the scene was one of horrific chaos. It was here that the privately owned 'small vessels' alerted by the Admiralty made history. Known later as the 'Cockleshell Navy' they came across the Channel in their thousands. Backwards and forwards they ferried, never giving up while there were still men to be picked up, they were credited with saving 90,000 of the 337,131 troops rescued from the beaches of France.

The country town where we lived was but a few miles from the English Channel and I can remember troop trains were arriving from the coast every few minutes, laden with soldiers direct from the fighting in France. Running through the streets we followed the crowds who were heading towards the station, eager not to miss the excitement.

On arrival we squeezed our way to the front of the crowd to see these returning warriors. Apart from one or two French or Belgian soldiers, they were all our 'boys' who had managed to escape from the holocaust that was Dunkirk.

The more seriously wounded stretcher cases were being taken away in ambulances, lorries and private cars. Many were groaning with pain from their wounds – some had died in the last few hours and were carried off the train, their faces covered. As they looked out from the carriage windows they seemed a tatterdemalion collection – some minus jackets, or boots or shirts, their clothing was still wet from the sea that had so nearly claimed them. Others – suffering from shell-shock, their entire bodies shaking, were sobbing uncontrollably like children.

Voluntary workers were handling steaming mugs of hot tea from an enormous silver urn (which seemed to be bottomless!) and platefuls of sandwiches through the train windows. It was amazing how good was the organization to enable the little town to deal with so many unexpected visitors. The small hospital could not cope with such large numbers of casualties and emergency rest centres were set up for the less serious cases in the Village Hall and even, I remember, in the single storey daughter church.

By now, the town was full of thousands of troops, those who were uninjured, roamed the streets where every door was open to them. People gave their all, inviting soldiers in for food, drink and even clothing for those who were in need. We talked with many men, asking childish questions about the war in France, and begged for souvenirs such as army buttons, badges and even in some cases live ammunition which they gladly gave. Many were still in a state of shock after the ordeal they had been through, their deep sunken eyes staring expressionlessly. God knows they had been through enough without being pestered by children, but we were too young to understand.

After a while no more troops arrived, in fact, within days it was difficult to find a soldier on the street. They were being shipped out to various destinations to be re-grouped for the battles that lay ahead. Life slowly returned to normal but the experiences of this time made a great impression on me. It was the first time in my life that I had ever seen real human suffering. The misery, the pain and perhaps more than anything, the blood made me think for the first time of the war as something greater than just an eruption in my way of life, and the excitement of battles reported in the news. I was at a very impressionable age and I had no one to turn to for comfort or a sense of security in my changing world. I think the characters of many youngsters must have been drastically affected during these years.

I think probably the most sympathetic character with whom I came in contact was Mrs Carpenter's father. He was a guard on the Southern Railway and he would pass our house nearly every day on his way home from the station. He lived in it little hamlet about one and a half miles away, and could take a short cut over the fields behind our house.

He had a snow-white bushy moustache – known, I believe, as a 'handlebar' moustache – and a thatch of white hair which stuck out from under his railway cap in all directions. He always carried the traditional guard's lamp of which he was inordinately proud, spending hours, I remember, cleaning and polishing it.

He was a dear old man and was very kind to me. Many was the time he brought me presents in the shape of objects left on the trains. Forage caps; army badges, naval caps and once a magnificent 'Sam Brown' belt, which should, of course, have been returned to some military H.Q., and which, afraid of its discovery, I kept in a cardboard shoe-box under my bed!

He used to tell me long rambling stories of his experiences when a child. He must have been a natural story-teller because everything he described came vividly alive and gave me a long-lasting impression of life in the days of Queen Victoria, when he was a boy.

He it was who persuaded my foster parents to allow me to keep a rabbit. I had always wanted a pet of my own but had never dared to ask – I knew that even Mrs Carpenter was willing, Mr Carpenter, with his strict ways and unbending attitude towards me would be adamant.

One Friday evening the three of them were sitting in the kitchen drinking tea as usual when I heard Mrs Carpenter's father say:

"Why don't you let the boy keep a pet? He's a lonely little chap – doesn't seem to have any real friends."

Mr Carpenter snorted.

"No good him having an animal, he'd never be home long enough to look after it – anyway couldn't afford it."

"Let him keep a rabbit – they don't cost nuthin' – eat green stuff mostly."

I couldn't hear the rest of the conversation because one of them shut the door, but one afternoon the next week Mrs Carpenter beckoned to me as I came in from school.

"Would you like to have a pet rabbit?"

I could hardly believe that her father had persuaded them.

"Yes, please!'"

"Well, you get the money and you shall. Old Mrs Moore down the road has some babies for sale and she can let you have an old hutch for half a crown."

I didn't need further bidding. A letter went off in the post to Mother and Father that evening, and by the end of the week I had the wherewithal for the rabbit and hutch.

Flopsy was a Flemish Giant, and I thought she was beautiful. Every day I would go down the lane with a large bag which I filled to overflowing with green stuff – mostly dandelion leaves, as Mrs Moore had told me this was rabbits' staple diet.

I don't know if she was wrong, or whether in my desire to keep Flopsy satisfied, I over-fed her, but the tragic end to the story was that one day about three months after I had so proudly brought her home, I went down to the hutch to feed her and found her stretched out, stiff and cold on the sawdust, blown up as fat and big as a football.

I buried her with great formality and even recited a prayer – learned under duress at school – as I shovelled the earth onto her poor bedraggled fur.

After this unhappy episode I think I became even more withdrawn. Flopsy's death affected me very deeply – I gave it more significance in my mind than was healthy. It seemed as if someone or something didn't intend that I should be happy and carefree like other boys. Although it was obviously my fault that I had lost her, I wanted to lay the blame elsewhere. I wanted to vent my anger and disillusionment on somebody else. I suppose it was the same old problem – I had no one to help and guide me through these traumatic childish – and later adolescent – experiences.

THE BLOODY "FROGGIES" HAVE CAPITULATED

"Never in the field of human conflict was so much owed by so many to so few."
Sir Winston Churchill, September, 1940.

It was on the way to school one morning in the middle of June, 1940, that we learned of the fall of France.

People in the streets were abusing the French for capitulating. The average Englishman had never been very 'pro' French, and expressions like "Bloody French"; "F...... Froggies" were heard frequently. One might have been forgiven for thinking these were the enemy, not the Germans!

On the 5th of June, the last part of the fight for France had begun. The Germans had held back a large section of their army during the evacuation of Dunkirk and they pressed upon the French defences between Paris and the sea. On 8th June they took Rouen. The seat of the French Government was moved from Paris to Tours and on 14th June the Germans took the capital.

I was beginning to get over the first pangs of home-sickness but I longed desperately to see my parents. John had settled down surprisingly well – perhaps because he was younger and more adaptable, or maybe because Mr and Mrs Carpenter obviously adored him. I had thought he would fret for Mother, but in fact I think it was I who lay awake at night wondering how she was faring.

I think I was already starting to become introverted. I had friends but no one really close to me. I was getting on quite well at school but still could not get involved in anything. However in August something happened that <u>did</u> fire my imagination – the Battle of Britain.
The Germans were launching a concerted air attack on southern England.
In a broadcast on 11th September, Winston Churchill stated ('Their Finest Hour'):

"Whenever the weather is favourable waves of German bombers, protected by fighters, often three or four hundred at a time, surge over this Island, especially the promontory of Kent, in the hope of attacking military and other objectives by daylight. However they are met by our fighter squadrons and nearly always broken up; and their losses average three to one in machines and six to one in pilots."

Much has been written of the gallantry of those fighter pilots, relentlessly beating back the enemy although hopelessly outnumbered, their indomitable courage giving hope to the old and firing the imaginations of the young. I wished passionately that I was old enough to join their ranks. They were the personification of the 'Young England' and the camaraderie and adulation with which they were surrounded must have given them an enormous feeling of transcendence that I envy even now. Known as 'The

Few' the pilots who fought the Battle of Britain were to become a legend. Young, brave, seemingly carefree, they fought in their Hurricanes and Spitfires for almost superhuman numbers of hours at a stretch. While on the ground waiting for their planes to be refuelled they were constantly on the qui vive – although appearing to be relaxed and unconcerned, the strain under which they lived was enormous.

The words 'Scramble! Scramble!' caused the airfield to burst into life at any time and the fighter planes would be airborne and combating the enemy in a matter of minutes.

From July until September the battle raged. There were never enough men – although our losses were slight in comparison with those of the enemy. Pilots could not be trained fast enough to replace those lost in action with the result that younger inexperienced men – hardly more than boys – were being sent up to fight this crucial battle.

On August 15th owing to the foresight of Air Marshal Dowding in holding in reserve a fighter force to guard the North, the Germans suffered their greatest losses when they attacked Tyneside with a force of 100 bombers escorted by 40 Me 110's. At the same time the usual daily attack on the south of England was carried out. Twenty-two of our squadrons fought two or sometimes three battles and the total German losses were 76 to our 34, in fact, in the northern raid 30 Heinkel 111's were destroyed for the loss of only two British!

By the end of August the Americans began to help us with their aircraft production but from then until the second week in September the British Fighter Command was almost paralysed by the destruction of nearly all the major airfields, making it impossible to get the planes into the air.

During the period August 24th – September 6th, 103 pilots were killed and 466 Spitfires and Hurricanes destroyed or seriously damaged.

On September 15th, one of the largest attacks on the south of England was launched and every squadron of British Fighters was engaged with none left in reserve. One hundred and eighty-three German planes were destroyed for the loss under 40 of our! With this magnificent battle the power of the German Luftwaffe was broken. The Battle of England had been won.

My parents like the vast majority of Londoners who had not been drafted into services, had stayed on and were enduring the almost daily bombing raids by the German Airforce. Adolf Hitler's intention was to break the morale of the civilian population by continuous day and night bombing attacks on British cities and towns. Young men and women were being conscripted into the armed forces with few exemptions. Unless you were fortunate to get into the fire-service or you were engaged in medicine there was little chance of your escaping the call of duty. My father was in his late forties and, therefore, was too old for service with the army. His eyesight was very poor and he had been a sick man for many years. It was extremely unlikely that he would be of much use in 'physically' fighting the enemy; even if he had volunteered, he would not have been accepted. By occupation he had been an antiquarian book-seller. The authorities considered his qualifications would be most useful at the Ministry of Information in London, to which he was assigned for the duration of the war. My mother, who was some ten years younger than my father, had been conscripted into the ambulance service. Never having even ridden a bicycle in her life, she was given a crash course and wrote us that she was now driving a two-ton ambulance. We also learned that she had part-time job as a waitress at London's fashionable Waldorf Hotel – not only for the hard cash it paid, but in wartime it was always possible to benefit gastronomically by working in a restaurant or hotel.

She would to tell us some amusing tales of her experiences. One which particularly appealed to me was the story of the Greek chef, father of seven, who invented some ingenious ways of getting out of the hotel with extra 'rations' for his family. His favourite trick was to tie a string around his middle (under his clothes) to which were tied choice pieces of steak. These were allowed to dangle down inside his trouser legs, completely invisible, of course, to the security guards outside the hotel! As he smilingly bade them "Good night," he would head for home with the family dinner.

The only means of contact with our parents was by writing, as telephoning was cut to the minimum for private calls were far too expensive. Special periods for letter-writing were included in the school time-table. How we looked forward to these letters from home. They were our only means of knowing that Mother and Father were alive and well, for although we felt sure that nothing could ever happen to them, we heard daily reports of the bombing of London and of the civilians who were being killed in their thousands.

Not a week went by without one or more of our classmates being informed that their mother, father or sometimes both had been killed in an air attack. It was invariably the impossible task for the teacher to break the news to the child. How did one start? A number on being told, had run away back to London to make sure their parents really were dead; they would not believe the news, thinking maybe it was a cruel joke or maybe someone had made a mistake...

I had now been away from home for a year and although I had accepted the fact that it <u>would</u> be a long time before I saw my parents again I was still homesick. I have said that I found school boring and the restrictions laid upon me by Mr and Mrs Carpenter irksome and suddenly with the summer holidays nearly here I began to be obsessed about seeing Mother and Father.

With opposition from everyone, I was determined that I would get away at all costs. I made everyone around me miserable with my tantrums, even threatening to run away if my parents would not visit me, or if I was not allowed to visit them. Mother and Father had obviously discussed the matter at length, and had finally agreed, after hearing from my headmaster at school that it would be better if I <u>did</u> visit, as he was sure I would run away if not.

A letter arrived saying I could return to the city but only for a few weeks during the summer holidays. In the letter was a second class ticket to London, which I was quick to notice, was a return ticket! Anyway, the important thing was that I had won. My campaign over the last few weeks had resulted in success and soon I would be on my way.

I made a calendar which I carried with me everywhere, sometimes waking up in the night to meticulously cross off another day. At school I boasted to my chums of my forthcoming trip, making them very envious. The thought of the journey; being in wartime London and sleeping in a shelter – which was one of the conditions – excited me so much that I could barely sleep as the day approached.

The day came, and hours before the train was due to arrive, I was ready. Dressed in my Sunday suit of grey flannel, my best school tie and cap and shoes as shiny as ebony, we left for the station. Strutting out, I hurried, almost ran to catch the train; it was quite unnecessary as I had all the time in the world. We waited half an hour or more before the train arrived. Quickly I boarded as Mr Carpenter placed my suitcase on the rack together with my coat, cap and paper bag which contained a snack for the journey – fish-paste sandwiches, biscuits and an apple. Slamming the door shut I pulled down the window with some effort so that I could lean out and wave goodbye to my foster parents as the train moved off. When they and the station were out of sight I pushed the window back up and sat down on the plush but rather stained velvet seat of the second class non-smoker where for the time being I was the only passenger.

My trip was quite uneventful – so different from that first journey south. The train was not an Express and I lost count of the number of times it stopped. All the names of the stations were blacked out – presumably so that if any Germans arrived by parachute (as was constantly expected) they would not know where they were.

At almost every station one or more passengers boarded the train and I amused myself by regarding them as unobtrusively as possible and making up stories about them. They all shared one characteristic – they looked tense and pre-occupied. Most of them were members of the Services - both men and women. I remember one couple – a Naval Officer and a young and pretty WRN. They sat in the far corner from me, their heads close together talking quietly and earnestly. He looked very much like my favourite film star – a man famous for his portrayal of 'Cloak and Dagger' characters and I remember I decided that he was off on a secret mission and was giving his companion details to report to MI5 or whoever his superiors might be in the event of his failure to return. My fantasy was substantiated when he left the train after about an hour at a small country station apparently miles from anywhere! Opposite me, for the latter part of the journey sat a middle-aged lady industriously knitting a large garment in khaki wool. She never stopped the whole time she was in the train – fingers flying, needles clicking. As she formed the stitches, her eyebrows went up and down in time.

I thought of my parents and wondered if they had changed – I knew I had. Thoughts kept flitting through my head as I sat gazing at the green countryside, the fields surrounded by neat hedges; the cattle grazing on the rolling hills – occasionally blotted out by the clouds of steam from the engine. My pocket watch, which I carried in my top jacket pocket – attached to the buttonhole for safety – I had checked at least two dozen times to see what progress we were making.

At last, I realised, we had reached suburban London with its endless rows of brick houses, stained black from a hundred years of city smoke. The countless chimney pots stretched as far as the eye could see. As the train made its final noisy stop, like the dying gasp of some giant beast, I lost not a second in opening the carriage door and with suitcase in hand, jumped out.

I stood on the platform eagerly scanning the crowds around the barrier. Suddenly I saw them. Dodging and pushing through the people alighting from the train I shoved my half-ticket into the collector's hand and hurled myself into my mother's arms.

When the first embraces were over and the incoherent questions: "How are you?" "How you've grown!" had abated a little, we found a taxi and started on the last leg of the journey home.

The first thing that struck me about my mother and father was that they looked much older than I remembered them. My father's hair was almost white and even my mother – who was much younger – had streaks of grey in her soft brown hair. They looked shabby too. My father's coat was patched at the elbows and even the patches were wearing thin, and my mother's dress was faded and shapeless. I think they had both lost a lot of weight which tended to make their clothes fall badly, and I think the tension of living in London had produced many wrinkles and lines of strain.

But however much they might have changed, they were still Mother and Father, and it was wonderful to be with them again.

"Do you get enough to eat?" my mother was asking. I told her, rather inarticulately I expect, how well Mrs Carpenter managed and about all the vegetables Mr Carpenter grew in the garden.

"That's something I should love to have – vegetables straight from the garden" said Mother. "Are you happy there? You sounded jolly desperate in your letters asking us to let you come home."

Looking back on the past months from this exciting environment made it all seem rather unreal.

"It's all right, I suppose."

I looked with interest out of the taxi window as we drove through the London streets. I was horrified by the scenes of devastation. The piles of rubble and twisted metal where bombs had exploded, and demolished buildings were to be seen everywhere. Other buildings, which had been fortunate to escape damage, had their windows covered either with curtaining which had been stuck to the glass, or else by brown sticky paper which had been criss-crossed to form a geometric pattern. The purpose of this was a precaution against flying glass.

I was struck by the fact that there were practically no children about, and by the sight of strange looking people in many different uniforms. There was hardly a civilian to be seen anywhere and those who were seemed to look terribly out of place.

There were Commonwealth soldiers from New Zealand, Australia and South Africa; colourful Indians; troops from Canada and the U.S., and many brave men and women who had escaped from Nazi-occupied Europe and formed their own forces, determined to return one day to liberate their homeland. London was as colourful and varied as a fairground and I found it fascinating. I was elated that I had triumphed in my determination to come back!

As we began to approach our home I could hardly contain my excitement and I wriggled about on the hard leather seat. My mother squeezed my hand.

"Soon be there."

Within a few moments we were paying off the taxi and I was running up the path to the front door. Once inside I looked around at the old familiar things. Nothing had changed and yet it seemed very different after my foster home. I leapt up the stairs to my bedroom. All my toys were just as I'd left them on that fateful morning so long ago.

Mother had emulated the Greek chef and had acquired a large rump steak from the Waldorf for our lunch – I could not remember ever having seen so much meat all in one piece. We fried it with onions and potatoes and it was delicious.

In the afternoon Father had to go back to work at the Ministry. Mother and I went first to do some shopping – something I quite enjoyed in spite of having to 'queue', for it was a thing I never did with Mrs Carpenter – and then I was taken to our next-door neighbours to be treated to more surprised exclamations of: "How you've grown!"

I was looking forward to going to bed. We were not going to sleep at home but were going to an Air-Raid Shelter. Little did I know what I was about to experience!

LONDON "BLITZ". LUFTWAFFE BOMBS DAY AND NIGHT

"Damage by enemy action stands on a different footing from any other kind of loss or damage"
Sir Winston Churchill, September 5th 1940.

By this stage of the war Londoners who had stayed on had adapted themselves to their new way of life, almost taking for granted that each day and night the German bombers would arrive for another attack on the city. The Luftwaffe was not only dropping high explosive bombs but also incendiary bombs which, dropped in their thousands turned London into a burning hell. There were also the mines, which dropped by parachute destroyed huge areas at a time. In the parks shelters had been built, and here during the long nights the Londoners slept, curled up in blankets waiting for the morning light. Basements and warehouses had also been converted into shelters but these could prove to be death traps if receiving a direct hit from a bomb. The most effective air-raid shelter however, was the London Underground and because of this, huge queues formed each night long before the gates were opened, of people from all walks of life, each carrying a bundle of bedding waiting patiently for sanctuary.
By now Londoners had learned to queue for practically everything. They waited neatly in line at the food shops for their turn to be served. Goods were not wrapped as no paper was available so shoppers either carried their own shopping bags or brought

newspaper with which to wrap their purchases. It was an accepted way of life and woe betide anyone who tried to 'queue jump'. This latter behaviour brought out the worst in the English temperament and often led to actual bodily assault. The crowds waiting to get into the subway were no exception and many a culprit was 'ousted' from the queue in the manner of a drunk from a public bar for not taking his turn.

I was amazed to see the size of the queue which we joined at about 6 pm. It was formed of people from all walks of life. City workers in their business clothes – including rolled umbrellas and bowler hats! – middle-class families, most of whose children clutched a teddy-bear, or some familiar and much-loved toy to comfort them during the long noisy night; society 'debs' many in long dresses and mink capes rubbing shoulders with large good-natured Cockney women whose natural wit was often the mainstay of the shelterers morale.

At a given moment – often the wailing of the air-raid siren which warned of approaching enemy aircraft, the gates of the subway were opened and the stampede began. Running like hunted deer, the mob descended elbowing their way down the steps to the catacomb-like safety of the platforms below. It was amazing how animal-like human beings became when raced with the struggle of survival. One night as we hurried along to the shelter because the air-raid siren had gone earlier than usual, we met my aunt – who lived in the next street – and her family doing likewise. Somehow we reached the steps to the subway together and to my utter astonishment my aunt stuck out her elbows and literally pushed my mother and me out of the way so that she and her two children could get to safety first.

My mother was so incensed at this behaviour I remember that she swore she would never speak to her sister-in-law again until she had apologised. After the war my aunt moved to California and the apology was never made!

First come, first served was the order of the day. The first few dozen took the few wooden bunks which were two or three deep and lined the platform wall, but the majority slept on the concrete platform contented to have even managed to get down below for each night many hundreds were locked out in disappointment. As it was, too many were always let into the subway so that not one square inch of the stone platform could be seen. Side by side, row by row they lay, each person huddled in a blanket or eiderdown, not two of matching colours, looking like a gargantuan human patchwork.

The stench in some of these overcrowded shelters was unbelievable; thousands of bodies living and sleeping side by side. Many had lost their homes and had no facilities for washing. The smell of sweaty bodies was appalling, this mixed with tobacco fumes, alcohol and stale urine can only be described as a cross between a jockey's changing room and a fertilizer factory on a sunny afternoon. The air at times was so thick you could have cut it with a knife. Still, all this was preferable to the alternative –

young, old, washed, unwashed, British, non-British, we were all in the same boat – bloody scared!

During the long nights below ground, impromptu entertainment was arranged. Amateur talent was encouraged; in fact, anyone who could do anything to help pass the tedious night was welcome. Some sang – or thought they could – and others tried to dance in the restricted space. There were accordion players, whistlers, spoon-players and magicians, most of whose talent left much to be desired. After a few nights we knew everyone's act by heart, but we were thankful for any form of diversion to take our minds off our immediate fears. Could we hold out? How long was this mole-like subterranean existence to continue?

Not all the entertainment in the shelters was third class; many professional musicians and other artists gave of their service unstintingly. I was privileged to be in the 'audience' on several occasions. We did not always go down to the Underground at night. My father's book shop was not doing very well at this time – who wanted to buy antiquarian books in time of war? Adventure stories and romantic novels were the order of the day for publishers – escapism was a necessary antidote to the stresses and strains. Father had leased a small newsagent and tobacconists situated between the YWCA and the YMCA in Great Russell Street. He supplemented his income from this by offering, for a small fee, to guard the bundles of bedding and valued possessions that people, going down into the shelters, did not wish to leave at home in case of looting which was rife at this time – particularly at night. Underneath the YMCA was a large basement which was converted into an air-raid shelter, and here we often used to take refuge. One night we were entertained by the playing of a blind pianist whom I learned later was the famous George Shearing. Friends had actually carried a piano down into the shelter and persuaded him to play. Every night he would give impromptu concerts which did much to allay the fears and raise the spirits of the shelterers.

The wit of the London Cockney is famous and sharp as a knife. Their sense of humour, which they never lost during the inhuman blitz of London, was their salvation in those terrible days.

During one of the worst attacks the exit to our shelter was opened a number of times to bring in civilians who had been injured. Some forty or fifty had been admitted, as roads were blocked with debris and no ambulances were available for the time being. It was some hours before help arrived and after the wounded had been carried out on stretchers, to be given medical attention, a warden on a routine check shouted from the entrance:

"Any injured or expectant muvvers in 'ere?"

A toothless old Cockney woman who must have been in her seventies replied:

"Give us 'alf a mo', mate…"

With their cry of 'We can take it' and the wartime mood of 'What's good enough for anybody's good enough for us,' the Londoners put up with the most incredible hardships.

Whenever the weather was favourable waves of bombers attacked London. Protected by fighters often as many three or four hundred at a time, they dropped their bombs, apparently indiscriminately, regardless of the lives of women and children.

At times the noise of the bombing was deafening, and the thud of each bomb exploding could be heard as it vibrated beneath the surface.

Come daytime, the shelters were cleared – everyone was evicted, regardless of whether they had a home to go to or not. Weary people climbed the steps up to the daylight – it was like emerging from a tomb – not knowing what transformation had been made during the night. Buildings which had stood the previous day were often now only piles of rubble – mounds of twisted metal and wood still smouldering, the whole mass looking like a volcano after an eruption.

At this time, Britain stood in very real danger of being invaded by Germany, and since his appointment as Prime Minister, Mr Winston Churchill had been urging the United States for:

"The loan of forty or fifty of your older destroyers to bridge the gap between what we have now and the large new construction we put in hand at the beginning of the war."

On July 31st, Churchill again cabled to President Roosevelt:

"It has become most urgent for you to let us have the destroyers, motorboats and flying boats for which we have asked..."

Britain and the United States then entered into negotiations for the transfer of these ships to the British Navy in exchange for the leasing of bases in the British Possessions in the West Indies. To quote Mr Churchill again:

"... the transfer of the destroyers to Britain in September, 1940, was an event which brought the United States definitely nearer to us and to the war, and it was the first of a long succession of increasingly unneutral acts in the Atlantic which were of the utmost service to us."

I was thoroughly enjoying my stay in London. I was not old enough to be scared by the bombing – at the age of 9½, being killed only happened to other people, never to you. At first I spent all my days with my mother who had leave from her ambulance driving although she still went every evening to the Waldorf. I realised subconsciously, I think, that although her feelings for me had not changed, she had had many experiences I had not shared. She was living such a different life to the one when she was just plain 'Mother' that inevitably I felt a little jealous of her other interests. I clung to her more than a boy of my age should, and made demands on her, particularly in the way of 'outings' which was difficult for her as not many forms of entertainment were open.

The Zoo at Regent's Park was a great favourite, I remember – I don't think it ever closed to the public. The Aviary, of course, was my chief venue of delight – I wished I could add the eggs of some of these exotic creatures to the collection I had just started. Sometimes we hired a boat on the Serpentine and I would row my mother across the lake, steering, I'm afraid, a rather erratic course but she never complained and on the sunny August afternoons it was a cool restful way to pass one's time. Riding on double-decker buses was an occupation of which I never tired – there were very few buses in the country and I don't think I ever rode in one the whole time I was evacuated. The view from the top of a double-decker was so different it made London seem like another world. Once we went to Kew Gardens and wandered for hours among the neatly tended beds of gaily coloured flowers but the most intriguing part of the visit for me was going into a hot-house and seeing real oranges and lemons growing. They made my mouth water because they were almost unobtainable in the shops. Eventually mother's leave expired and she had to return to duty as an ambulance driver. Then I spent my days with my father and came to know him better, I think, than ever before.

He had always been a cheerful optimistic person, although tending to have what one would call a certain amount of 'artistic temperament', I suppose. His great love was writing, seconded by collecting rare and beautiful books. He loved beautiful things and often when shown a sordid scene or a hideous block of buildings would point out unerringly one or more saving graces.

Generous to a fault, he was always willing to give anyone in need his last penny and delighted to buy a drink for anyone – even a complete stranger if he took a fancy to them. Immensely popular, I think everyone loved him.

Father was entirely impractical having no head for business at all – in fact he had never learned a trade. His education had been interrupted by the First World War and he had tried many jobs before deciding to work in a publishing firm as he felt it would further his writing interests. From then he had worked his way up slowly until the firm went bankrupt by which time he had married my mother and I was on the way.

His next employment was in a book shop which eventually led to his specialization in antiquarian books.

I think I discovered at this time that Father wasn't perhaps as carefree and happy as he made out. He often reminisced about his life and such phrases as "What I should have done was…" and "If I had my time again I'd do things differently…" made me realise that he did yet think of himself as anything but a failure with nothing to offer his wife and children in the future – little did he know it but he was going to have a good deal less very shortly.

Waves of Heinkels escorted by Messerschmitts continued to drop their bombs on London. Day in, day out. Night after weary night we heard the wailing of the air-raid sirens and the drone of the bombers. Power was cut off together with the water supply and terrible damage was done to property. In all, during a nine months' period, 40,000 people were killed and more than 120,000 wounded in air attacks.

It was on one morning – a morning that was to change our lives for many years to come – that we reached the street after yet another night in the subway. The air smelt cool and sweet as we breathed deeply. Once again the sky was above us, as we slowly walked towards home, carrying our bedding. The scene was a familiar one – of people living up to the famous slogan - "Business as usual!" Shopkeepers were clearing up broken glass and debris from the pavements. Pieces of masonry, timber and rubble were being swept from the streets by workmen, and a London taxi, battered and upturned onto its roof, blocked the road like a giant beetle which had somehow got on its back and couldn't right itself.

As we turned the corner, we could scarcely believe our eyes; an entire row of houses had completely disappeared. What had been a block of some twenty houses was now a smouldering mountain of rubble; the entire block had collapsed – not a door or window remained. A few hours before one of these houses had been our home. We learned later that it had received a direct hit from an aerial landmine – the type the Luftwaffe dropped by parachute – and had collapsed like a pack of cards leaving only the shell.

The day was spent climbing over the rubble, salvaging what we could. Mother quietly wept much of the time as we searched like scavengers. We found a shoe, Father's Dunhill pipe, a broken teapot. The weak sun shone through the holes in the shattered walls which were once windows, casting shadows on us as we clawed amongst the broken bricks in the hope of finding something which could be used. Our hands were raw, stained red from the bricks as we laboured on towards evening. During this day no one had stopped to ask us if they could help us – but then why should they? This was no unusual happening but an everyday occurrence, and here we were like dogs on the street – hungry and homeless.

I do not remember the passing of time - I suppose we spent all day searching the ruins, but as it began to get dark Father made us give up and we wandered rather aimlessly along the streets until we came to an Emergency Post. This had been a School and miraculously was undamaged. Organizations like the Salvation Army ran their posts and provided mobile food units for people like us who suddenly found themselves with nothing. We checked in and were given steaming mugs of hot tea which we drank ravenously cradling our hands round the china to gain some comfort.

After we had finished our tea an ARP (Air Raid Precaution) Warden beckoned my father over to a desk in one corner or the room. Complete with steel helmet, dark-belted raincoat and gas mask slung over one shoulder he sat down on one side of the desk and my father on the other.

"What type of property has been affected, sir?"

My father, grey-faced with exhaustion, looked at him blankly.

"Has your home been bombed?" the warden explained patiently – he must have become accustomed to dealing with people suffering from shock, I suppose. My father nodded.

"Has it been completely demolished?" Again my father nodded. I was afraid everyone would think he was drunk, he seemed so dazed.

"Were any lives lost?"

At last my father spoke. "No, thank God"

The warden went on asking questions and filling in a form on the desk. At last when two pages had been filled he put down his pen and got up. "We can't find accommodation, sir, I suggest you spend the night in the shelter, but if you want food and hot drinks tomorrow, come back here – if we're still here," he added quietly as simultaneously the air-raid siren began to wail and a load of bombs whistled down not far away.

We hurried to the nearest Underground where we slept the night through, utterly and completely exhausted.

The next day we set out to try to find somewhere to live. We were incredibly lucky for an old friend of Father's offered us the use of his basement.

Although it was small, with a window looking onto a courtyard below street-level, it was a blessing. There was also a gas-ring to cook on, running water and, most important, a roof over our heads. I knew my "holiday" was at an end and that I must return to the country away from this horror and devastation, while my parents tried to reorganise their lives.

Luckily I still had my return ticket and I had not brought much in the way of luggage so its loss was negligible.

It was with a heavy heart I boarded the train to return to my foster parents and this time I clung to my mother as we said goodbye.

A NEW SCHOOL – SADISTIC TEACHERS

"Come then, let us go forward together with our united strength."
Sir Winston Churchill, 1940.

Before leaving on my eventful trip to London I had sat for a school examination. It was the system at the time to give a limited number of free scholarships to outstanding students which enabled them to go to a 'better' school – a school which took mainly private paying students. On my return I learned that I had won a scholarship to the local school. This was a rare honour as few students were accepted on this basis at the school in question. Schooling was virtually free but there were considerable other expenses involved. My parents in their present plight, were not in a position to assist financially but I was told a grant had been given to me from the local educational authorities, and the other expenses my foster parents would pay for the time being.

The school outfitters was at the far side of the town and on the day of our visit we left the house at 9 a.m.

"I do hope they will have everything in your size," said Mrs Carpenter. "We are so late getting you fitted up, what with you being away and all."

The shop when we eventually arrived was a large impressive place. Once inside the door we were met by a gentleman in grey pin stripe trousers and a black jacket who after solemnly inquiring to which school I was bound, ushered us past shelves of shirts, pullovers and blazers of varying colours to a counter over which a gold coat of arms proclaimed the motto of my new school.

I was taken in charge by an elderly gentleman who walked with a permanent stoop and whose voice barely vibrated his vocal chords and I found his whispered conversation exceedingly trying during the next hour or so.

First we bought two grey shirts, two vests, three pairs of pants and four pairs of grey socks. Then came the more interesting part. The school uniform consisted of a grey suit with blue piping round the lapels and cuffs and a grey and blue striped tie. The tie was easy, the jacket fitted perfectly, but the trousers! I looked like the back half of a 'property donkey' from a pantomime. This was because although fairly broad-shouldered, I had very narrow hips and a small waist. The assistant shook his head and sucked in his breath. "That won't do," he whispered, "that won't do at all, young sir." He shuffled away and was absent for what seemed hours. Eventually he returned with two more pairs of trousers. These we proceeded to try. All in vain – one was too small even for me, the other too short in the leg. We had come to an impasse.

Up to this point I had been enjoying the break from routine but now I began to fidget.

"Keep still," Mrs Carpenter commanded. I obeyed. After much discussion and misery it was decided we would have to have the short ones and let them down for the school term commenced the following week and there was no more time to order more.

Next I had to try on school caps – a must for every British schoolboy and here we also had trouble as they were either so big they rested on my ears, or so small they perched on the top of my head like a pimple. This really would have to be ordered specially for me and I realised with dismay that I should have to start my new school minus my cap! That great status symbol.

We were not finished yet for I had to have football shirts, shorts, socks and boots and a pair of long white trousers for cricket. At long last, weary, frayed and hungry, we emerged from the shop. As it was by now lunchtime, Mrs Carpenter suggested we go to the British Restaurant, fortunately only a few yards away. These restaurants were the only eating places open – in country districts anyway during wartime – the restrictions of rationing preventing the running of cafes. Run by the Government, they provided a plain but well-balanced meal for the price of one shilling and sixpence.

Having been 'kitted out' there was only one problem left regarding my entry into a new school – namely means of transport. It was even further than the old one from my home and there were no buses because of the strict rationing of petrol. Obviously, I required a bicycle. I wrote to my father telling him of my need saying that all the other boys had bicycles on which to ride to school. This was not strictly true, and looking back I realise how selfish it was of me to expect my father, having just lost everything he possessed in the destruction of his home, to set about finding the means or money to obtain a bicycle for me. It shows, I think, to what extent I had become self-centred – demanding as my right, compensation for being exiled from my beloved London. I knew that I had been sent away for my own good but felt rejected and that the good clean home Mr and Mrs Carpenter had made for John and me was 'second best'.

I shall never know how my father managed it but within a few days I received an official notification, addressed to me personally stating that the Southern Railway was holding a bicycle which had been sent from London at the local station.

I collected it the same day. Running like a dog after a hare I covered the two miles to the station in record time clutching the claim form in my hot hand.

I was as proud as a peacock as I wheeled away this latest acquisition. It was a little rusty, of course, as it was second-hand, but it had dropped 'racing-type' handlebars and to my adoring eyes looked perfect.

That weekend was spent putting it in first class order. I mended the two punctures – holding the inner tubes in a bowl of water as instructed by Mr Carpenter, pleased to find me with an interest at last – watching for the tell-tale bubbles that would indicate where the air was escaping. I polished the chrome until it shone like silver, and oiled every nut and bolt I could reach. At last it was ready.

My new school was a great disappointment. I don't know quite what I had been expecting – something that would catch my interest and give me a feeling of involvement, I suppose.

Every schoolboy will recall the helpless and lonely feeling of the first day at a new school; the complete and utter strangeness of everything as the older boys hurry confidently about their business along the noisy corridors. These 'oldens' looked at us as if we were inhabitants from another planet, and the terrifying superiority of the prefects and masters in their priest-like black gowns seemed to symbolise the necessity for obedience and discipline.

Prayers were held every morning in the big hall where with the arrival of the headmaster we froze in silence as if in the presence of the Messiah.

This then was to be my life for the next few years and I am afraid I spent more time rebelling than learning; where days were measured by the hours one sat awaiting the sound of the final bell which meant another day was over. School was an evil necessity where I was to make few friends, either amongst the other students or amongst the teachers.

Memories of the masters are not very pleasant ones and my main recollection is that they seemed persons full of their own importance, drunk with the power which they had been given over their helpless charges, teaching through fear not inspiration and lacking the kindness and understanding to teach by example. They, no doubt, had all the qualifications together with all the academic degrees from the best Oxford and Cambridge Universities, but were still unable, through their Victorian methods of teaching, to create by warmth of personality a genuine interest in the subjects they taught. The system of teaching was one of a superior talking down to sub-standard beings who should feel fortunate for this opportunity they were being given.

Many of the masters were in the wrong profession and should never have been allowed to be in such a position, entrusted with teaching and moulding the minds of the young. Others were obvious sadists – some mental and others physical – who made no attempt to camouflage their perverted feelings; and there were those with obvious homosexual tendencies.

French and Latin were taught from a very early age together with other normal subjects. Already, at the age of ten, a number of periods each week were devoted to French and were taught by a youngish man who, although he had a French name, appeared to be English. Very full of his own importance he considered himself very humorous and specialised in sarcastic wit – never missing an opportunity to humiliate verbally a student whom he disliked. Little time was spent in French conversation – the lesson was taught by repetition. It is no wonder the English have the distinction of being the world's worst linguists.

During the lesson, 'mon professeur' would strut up and down the classroom, carrying a ruler with which he swatted boys over the head. This instrument of flagellation he referred to as his 'Excalibur' and with it he conducted the lesson using it like a baton in the hands of an orchestral conductor. At frequent intervals he would leave the rostrum to administer a hearty whack on a boy's head for not paying attention and sometimes used the broad side of the ruler on a boy's skull if he was feeling in a particularly vicious mood.

Unlike a normal lesson when there is relative silence in the classroom, the collective chanting during the French lesson gave us the opportunity to amuse ourselves in a variety of ways to relieve the boredom. The firing of paper clips in the class and the less lethal blotting-paper ball which could be fired with the aid of the forefinger and thumb and a rubber band (after first being dipped in the ink-well!) were favourites. Breaking wind in class was also a skilful pastime. Timing and complete control were needed – loud enough for your classmates to hear but out of earshot of the teacher!

Of all the boys, one was in a class of his own and was the acknowledged champion. He could amuse us for hours with his impersonations, until our sides ached and tears were running down our cheeks. Announcing prior to the performance that now he would produce a sound of 'a baby crying for its mother' or 'the ripping of a canvas sail in a storm' or 'a howling dog' he would then proceed to reproduce these sounds in a most realistic manner. His greatest feat was a very recognisable version of the first few bars of 'Rule Britannia'!

Corporal punishment could only officially be administered by the headmaster and for minor misdemeanours the masters awarded detentions. This meant staying at school for an extra hour, or returning on a free afternoon during which time it was left to the discretion of the master as to whether we should be given work or condemned to sit in total silence for the period. If one was foolish enough to earn three or more detentions in anyone week, a visit to the headmaster ensued. Sitting sternly behind a huge mahogany desk he would remind us of our transgressions as he recounted them from an impressive register where our sins were recorded in detail. We would wait in dread for the verdict which could mean three, six or even a dozen strokes from a supple bamboo cane. Bent over a desk, the caning would leave stripes on our backsides which could last for anything up to two weeks, turning a variety of colours from red to purple and finally becoming a yellow-green bruise. An expert at flagellation, the Head punished with such accuracy that he could strike the same spot twice making the experience doubly painful.

Although the school ruling was that only the headmaster could hand out physical punishment, this was not adhered to and a variety of methods were used by the other masters – each having his own favourite method. One of the most hated teachers, a somewhat bloated looking Welshman with a vile temper, was the mathematics master. One day in a fit of temper he struck a boy so hard that he fell over, striking his head on a metal stove. The injuries were such that the child had to have a number of stitches in the wound. Much to our delight after this particular incident the man disappeared – rumour having it that at last he'd gone too far and had been dismissed. We never found out the truth of the matter.

Of all the teachers, our science master was the most eccentric and unpredictable in his behaviour. He was a short man with steel-grey hair which was cut close to his head, looking like fuse wire standing on end. He would enter the classroom sometimes shouting and raving for no apparent reason, but always. on the same theme:-

"You all need. to be flogged!" or "Young fellows should be horse-whipped!"

No doubt he derived some sadistic satisfaction as we sat, scared as rabbits, waiting for the storm to subside.

Few of us wore long trousers, but those who did were fortunate. The punishment for not paying attention in class was a vicious strike from this man's hand on the inside of the thigh. He could use such force that the imprint of his hand complete with fingers would be left on the boy's leg.

There were other teachers who had more subtle methods of punishment – one favourite being to make the culprits hold books above their heads for long periods – this I believe, is derived from an ancient Chinese form of torture.

The sports activities were plentiful and there was a variety of instruction in all kinds of physical activity. Soccer, rugby, and cricket were taught and many hours were spent in the gymnasium doing P.T. All these sports and exercises were carried out under the watchful eye of an ex-sergeant-major who had taught physical instruction in the army. Now very much overweight and possessing a pot-belly, he had no doubt been a fine physical specimen in his earlier days. His great pride was his traditional army moustache – carefully waxed each day. At frequent intervals he would twiddle the ends with his forefinger and thumb. It was not difficult to understand why he was nicknamed 'Waxey' by the boys, who liked him generally in spite of his military manner of bellowing his instructions at the top of his very powerful voice. Cross-country runs were organised, even in sub-zero temperatures; with only running shorts and vest we would set off through the country lanes, while Waxey followed on his bicycle – a sheepdog herding his flock!

Sometimes it was possible to slip away a few minutes after leaving the school grounds. By rolling into a ditch or hiding in a hedge, one could watch smugly while the others disappeared in the distance, their voices growing rapidly fainter. The thrill of having escaped from this boring activity gave one a wonderful feeling of superiority. The time was passed congratulating ourselves on our achievement and sitting in a circle puffing away at cigarette ends secreted in the pockets of our shorts. Coughing and spluttering we would pass the butt round from mouth to mouth, no one daring to refuse in case they were labelled 'coward'. Here we would wait, often becoming stiff with cold, until we heard the pounding of feet and knew our classmates were returning. As they passed our hiding place, we would leap out into the open and join their exhausted band for the last hundred yard dash back to school.

Cricket was played. in the summer regardless of weather, and on occasions a sudden downpour would send us running for the pavilion, our neatly creased white trousers now a shapeless mess – heavy, wet and very uncomfortable. The game would be postponed, not for the benefit of the players, but to preserve the pitch which had been rolled and flattened until it was as smooth and green as a billiard table. Of all the sports played in 'good' English schools this, to me, was the most boring. Apart from the few players who at one time are engaged in action during the match the remainder pass most of the game waiting tediously for something to happen. It is no wonder that no American, nor for that matter anyone who does not happen to be British, has ever been able to fathom out either the object of the game nor the reason why it has such a keen following.

Regardless of our preferences all students had to participate in all sports, and by far my personal preference was soccer, at which it was said I excelled. We played inter-class matches as well as against other school teams. As soon as the soccer season started in the autumn, most evenings were spent practising for long hours on any field and with any ball that could be kicked. Fog, rain, nothing would deter us as long as there was sufficient light to see the ball. Soccer was the only thing that made my schooldays bearable. Playing, I could lose myself completely and was no longer the bitter cynical onlooker at life – I was involved, part of something worthwhile. If one of the masters had only taken the trouble to notice what was going on and had taken me in hand my life might have turned out very differently.

As is the custom in English schools, work was taken home every night and could be two, three or even four subjects, each one taking about half an hour. By now we were getting three subjects per night which meant much of the evening was spent working, leaving little time for football. I am afraid I fell into the questionable habit of leaving my work until I reached school next morning and hoping someone more assiduous than I would let me copy what he had done. This was obviously the quickest but not the safest way!

It was on one of these mornings that I arrived at school only few minutes before the bell went for morning prayers. Dismounting from my bicycle I hurried across the playground to the bike shed and grabbing my satchel scanned the surrounds for someone from whom I could copy my 'homework'. Luckily I found a classmate who agreed to let me do as I wished, and we hurried towards the latrines – the safest place to hide that we could think of in the time. Nervously huddled in a corner I started to copy the page of algebra, scribbling as fast as I could. I had nearly completed the task when my eyes suddenly focussed on a pair of highly-polished shoes, and the hem of a black gown. Raising my eyes in horror I met those of the Headmaster. I gasped, dropped my pencil which quickly floated away on a stream of urine, and waited, trembling.

"Go and wait outside my study."

"Yes, sir."

Minutes later we were standing outside his door like prisoners awaiting execution, my friend cursing me for getting him involved, and both knowing full well that nothing could save us from a beating.

Finally, he arrived and we were beckoned into the study. After a lecture on how disappointed my father would be to learn I had been cheating, I was told to bend over the desk, whereupon I received 'six of the best'. The other boy, who after all was only an accessory to the crime, got off with a nicely phrased homily on the varying aspects of honour.

As I recall the waiting and the lecture were much worse than the caning, but it was a very unpleasant experience, and after this I made sure, that I was never caught again.

By now my London accent had been lost and I spoke with a distinct southern accent – a slow lazy manner of talking, sounding as if one had a hot potato in the mouth. My school mates still referred to me as 'cockney' or 'evacuee' which did nothing to help any form of integration. Apart from me, there was only one other 'foreigner' – a German Jew who must have suffered terribly from the taunting and open Anti-Semitism of the other boys. I don't think a day went by without an incident of some sort or another to remind him he was not one of 'them'. Because of this I felt more drawn to him than anyone else, but we never really became more than amicable acquaintances. I suppose it was only natural that these local boys, whose families had lived in the town for generations should consider that anything outside their 'little world' was strange and foreign, but it all added fuel to the fire of my rebelliousness.

HESS DEFECTS – DOG FIGHTS

"Do your worst and we will do our best."
Sir Winston Churchill, 1941.

Everything was now in short supply in wartime Britain – food, clothing, school teachers and even instrumentalists for the local Brass Band! I learned from some school friends that there was to be an audition in the Salvation Army Hut in order to recruit schoolboys to supplement the Band's depleted numbers, and although I could not play an instrument, I decided to go along. The hut was situated in the centre of the town – it was used for a variety of functions – Jumble Sales, Flower Shows, Boy Scout meetings and also on occasions end of term concerts by my old school so I was familiar with the layout.
I went in and sat down with some dozen or so boys whose age ranged from about seven to fourteen. Eventually the Bandmaster, a tall man of about sixty who had snow-white hair and bushy eyebrows came up to us and started to ask us questions.
"Can any of you play any instrument?"
We all shook our heads. He did not seem unduly worried.
"Can any of you read music?"
Two boys nodded their heads – it transpired they learned the theory of music at school. For some reason the old man then came up to me.

"Why do you want to join my band?" – I looked into his piercing blue eyes and racked my brains for a sensible answer, not liking to say that it had really been on impulse.

"Please sir, I like music and I would like to learn to play something."

He nodded, apparently satisfied. He was, I found out as the weeks went by, a very patient man and a dedicated musician, and nothing was too much trouble to explain once he had decided his pupil was genuinely interested.

There was no choice of instrument – we were given whatever was available. The boy in front of me drew a euphonium, a large three-valved silver thing which was not only cumbersome to carry but also needed much puffing to produce a sound out of it. I was more fortunate and was given an instrument, slightly bigger than a cornet which I was told was a flugelhorn. This was also silver – many of the instruments were, which seemed strange in a brass band – and was pitched, I learned later in the key of B flat. I was very proud of it.

Alter a few minutes instruction we were told to go home and practise blowing long notes – nothing else - and to return the following week at the same time and the same place to see how we had progressed.

"Do not, I repeat NOT blow your instruments in the streets, my boys," were his parting words to us. "You may think you are making music but the people hearing you will complain to the council of the terrible caterwauling and then where will my budding bandsmen be!"

Needless to say in spite of these words of warning the temptation was too much to resist and producing hideous sounds we marched through the unlit streets blowing until we were scarlet in the face! As the weeks passed I began to make progress. I discovered that I had an aptitude for music and what is more I really enjoyed playing.

This was the only activity – other than soccer – in which I participated with other people and did not feel an 'outsider'.

At each weekly meeting I was given an hour's tuition, then sent home to practise until the next session. I could now play scales and even simple pieces in the key of C. A band uniform had been presented to me which had yards of gold braid round the blue cloth of cuffs, collar and epaulettes. The trousers had a magnificent gold stripe down the side and to crown it all there was an officer's type hat which was so big it was necessary to pack strips of newspaper around the interior to make it stay on my head. In this outsize outfit, looking like a miniature field-marshal, I joined the rest of the musicians each week for practise.

As the months went by, we newcomers became more proficient and occasionally we would be allowed to join in public appearances in the park on Sunday afternoons. At first, sitting in the circular bandstand I was so nervous and so afraid I would make a mistake that all my practising was wasted for hardly a sound came from my instrument as I manipulated the valves without blowing in an attempt to fool the onlookers. But gradually I gained confidence and 'did my bit' with the rest of them. It was an experience I shall be grateful for all my life.

My free time at weekends and after school and the weeks of the vacation from school, I spent out of doors whenever possible, spending less and less time with my foster parents as time went by. I looked forward to the long summer evenings when, unrestricted by the adult world, I could wander at will through the peaceful forests, and wind-swept hills of the English countryside. It was only on these occasions that I felt really free.

I busied myself fishing in the crystal clear streams or collecting eggs from the cunningly concealed birds' nests, hidden like stars in the thick hedges and trees. My collection of birds' eggs was soon the finest and most varied that any schoolboy could have wished for. All carefully labelled and stored in shoe-boxes which were lined with cotton wool, each showed the type of egg, together with the location and date it had been acquired.

I soon learned that the blue tit's nest can be found in the moss-lined hollows of fruit trees, that the skylark, whose sweet trilling song bubbled away constantly on summer days, built her nest on the ground, in long tussocky grass, and when she alighted from the sky above she would drop some several feet away so that any predator would not know the nest's exact location.

In the marshland I found many moorhens' eggs – sometimes as many as fifteen or sixteen at one time – which were edible and as far as I can recall very good, although rather rich. Nevertheless they were a welcome addition to the meagre ration of hens' eggs which was, at this period, one per person per week.

Relaxing dreamily on the river banks, I would sit for hours watching the kingfishers burrowing out earth to make their nests in which to lay their beautiful pink eggs, or flashing like blue fire across the water to dive for minnows on which to feed their young (who were sometimes smaller than the food they were fed!).

The squawking black rooks built their nests at the top of the very tallest trees where the branches were frequently brittle and withered. This presented a challenge for only the bravest. The slow climb to the top, brittle bough by brittle bough, at each step there was a snap like breaking glass beneath one's shoe. Then the careful insertion of hand into nest to grope for the egg which when lifted out was placed delicately in the mouth while the descent was made – it was much too difficult an operation to accomplish one-handed. I remember one such climb, rook's egg in mouth, ending in a small disaster. About five feet from the safety of the ground, I slipped and fell flat on my face. Luckily the ground was very soft from rain the night before, but the jolt to my head caused me to clench my teeth violently, thereby crushing to powder the precious egg. As for the taste, I didn't know it but the nest had been abandoned and the eggs had become addled. It took a long time before I could stomach even an innocent hen's egg (a great luxury in wartime) for breakfast.

To remove the fluid from an egg was no job for the inexperienced, needing a lot of puff and a steady hand. A neat hole was made with a matchstick at either end of the egg then you put it to your mouth and blew. On some occasions the egg was addled and no amount of puffing or blowing would help.

In Southern England the shallow streams abound in trout and other fish, on a summer's afternoon, I would go 'spearing'. A simple piece of equipment was used, consisting of a stick about three feet in length, and an old fork which had been well-sharpened, and attached to the stick with either string or a piece of wire. This made a primitive but very effective weapon for catching fish. Armed with this pronged-spear, we went on our fishing expeditions for trout. With trousers rolled up above my knees, standing in the crystal-clear water, I would spear fish until my legs were blue from the icy water. Sometimes returning with a dozen or more unfortunate trout.

The farmers in these times were desperately short of labour as most of their help had been conscripted into the service. To fill the need for farm help an organization called the 'Land Army' was .formed, consisting of a force of volunteers who were in most cases young ladies who joined as an alternative to being drafted into one of the armed forces. They were, in most cases, from 'good' families being rather bucksome and looking the picture of health in their farm uniforms which the authorities issued them. This consisted of a heavy-knit khaki pullover, riding-breeches and knee-length boots to protect them from the mud and muck of the farmyard. I do remember at the time the many stories about these 'land girls' – of their sexual appetites and of the fun and frolics that went on between them and the many German and Italian prisoners who worked on the farms. Even some of our older schoolmates boasted that, at the weekends when they worked on the farms for pocket money, they had been literally introduced to the wonders of sex by these 'love-hungry lassies'. Whether there was any truth in these stories or not, there were many of them going around.

On long summer evenings and at weekends the farmers paid schoolboys to help in various ways, which was great fun and for us meant extra pocket money. In the potato-picking season we followed the tractor for long hours as it ploughed through the black earth like a slow ship rolling from side to side on a rough sea - churning up the seemingly endless crop of potatoes hidden beneath the surface. Following the line of the plough, we stooped sometimes from eight in the morning until lunch-time without stopping, chatting with our colleagues as we filled the large wicker baskets, which in turn were emptied into a lorry. For this back-breaking job we were paid sixpence an hour and, if the farmer was pleased with our work, we would be given a rabbit as a bonus, together with an invitation to return the next week. The rabbit would be taken home and roasted for the Sunday lunch, the skin we would take to a dealer, for which we would be paid three-pence.

Probably the most pleasant job was helping with the grain harvest. The cutting and binding had been done by experienced farmhands but, after the sun had dried the golden sheaves of corn, we would be entrusted to gather them up from the fields.

Leaving the farmyard, a team of five or six of us would ride atop a huge cart drawn by one or sometimes two horses and, armed with pitch-forks we would take it in turns to either pitch or stack. Catching the sheaf just below the cord which held it together, it needed strength and skill to toss it up onto the cart, especially when it was stacked high with sheaves; by the end of a day's work our hands were blistered and red-raw from the smooth wooden handle of the fork, worn as smooth as a beechnut shell from countless years of use.

An easier job was stacking the sheaves, as they were tossed onto the cart, stacking neatly with the ears of corn inwards. the load would get higher and higher and, as the cart slowly moved along, it became more and more wobbly. On occasions when a poor job of stacking had been done, the load would fall off. Amid laughter, we would work like miners in a landslide to load up the cart again before the farmer appeared, which would mean either dismissal or a deduction of our meagre earnings for the day. Gloves, for some reason, were never worn – either they were too cumbersome to work with or it had not occurred to us to wear them to protect our hands from the dried stinging nettles which grew amongst the corn and pierced our fingers like needles. The pay was good for casual farm work and was between six- and nine pence an hour for schoolboys; the amount was not a fixed rate but depended on how desperate or how generous the farmer was. We were nevertheless delighted with our earnings which for a full day's work meant going home with five or six shillings which to us was a vast fortune!

One of the less exciting jobs – and incidentally less lucrative – was 'docking' for which we were paid a miserable threepence an hour. Up and down the muddy fields we would tramp, our boots weighing what felt like a ton with the clayey soil clinging round the soles, looking for these obnoxious weeds called docks. It was the roots that did the damage apparently, smothering the roots of the crops and taking all the nutriment from them. They had to be dug out with a knife and lined up like a mine-detecting squad, knives at the ready we moved slowly forward, eyes cast down accompanied by a farmhand who gave us hell if we ever missed one. It was a monotonous job which I tried to avoid whenever I could.

It was about this time that I had two 'exciting adventures'. A young German airman whose plane had been hit in a dog fight not far away had bailed out of his machine and descended by parachute into a field near the next village. He was sent by train to our town where the county constabulary had its head-quarters. I rushed to the station together with many other excited children to gawk at this foreign invader. There he stood on the platform, handcuffed to a member of the local Home Guard – a voluntary, para-military force consisting of local men who were either too old for, or deferred from the armed services, with the prime objective of harassing or delaying an invader until such time as regular units arrived on the scene. This member looked very proud of the job delegated to him – that of playing jailor and escorting this gentleman from the Luftwaffe to prison camp.

The blond, blue-eyed German youth looked so normal. I had somehow expected him to look different. Possibly with a shaven head or Boris Karloff type features! I was very disappointed.

The other adventure occurred when I was out on one of my birds' nesting expeditions. It was a lovely tranquil day and the sudden droning of aircraft engines and the staccato sound of machine-gun fire in the distance broke rudely upon my solitude. Climbing a grassy knoll, I looked to the east and could see in the distant sky a dog fight – German bombers who, at this time, were launching a series of 'hit-and-run' daylight attacks – being chased by our Hurricanes and Spitfires.

I watched fascinated for such scenes were rare in our part of the country. It was quite a long way off so I was in no danger from falling shrapnel but suddenly I saw a plane descending in a nose-dive. Spiralling, spinning with smoke pouring from its tail it was headed in my direction! What should I do? My sense of distance was not very developed and I had visions of it crashing on top of me.

I flung myself down on the ground and minutes later there was a sickening thud, which shook the ground beneath me, followed by an explosion. After a few terrified minutes I raised my head. About half a mile away I could see pieces of aircraft fuselage scattered about.

Luckily I had my bicycle with me and hastily retrieving it from where I had flung it, I rode as fast as I could over the bumpy ground to the scene of the crash. It was an appalling mess. Of the pilot there was no trace. I was disappointed about this as, riding across to the crash I had been imagining him crawling out of the burning wreckage – as in many films I had seen – and me going to his rescue, and later handing him over to the authorities! He must have been blown to bits.

After about twenty minutes, some members of the Home Guard arrived driving at a frantic pace on a farm tractor.

"Did you see it come down, lad?"

I nodded, feeling very important and gave an account of what I had seen. They' looked solemn. "Poor young feller – even if he was a 'Jerry' he was someone's husband or son."

I, of course, had not given a thought to such things. To me it was the most exciting thing that had ever happened to me.

It was about this time that Rudolf Hess flew into Scotland with his wild plan for peace.

He had been a favourite of Adolf Hitler while on his personal staff before the war, but when the pressures of war increased and the Fuehrer had less time for social activities, Hess felt that he was no longer popular with his idol. He conceived a plan to bring himself back into the limelight. He decided that it was Churchill and the British Government that were the true enemies of Germany and that he, Rudolf Hess, would go to the King of England himself and make peace.

His political advisor Albrecht Haushofer had met the Duke of Hamilton – who was now Lord Steward – at the 1936 Olympic Games and on this slender thread of presumed acquaintanceship Hess piloted his own plane from Augsburg and parachuted down within ten miles of the Duke's home in Dungavel, leaving the aircraft to descend where it might. He was arrested and taken to a military hospital in Glasgow to have the superficial wounds sustained on his landing attended to. His story was so far-fetched that he was also examined by a psychiatrist who conceded that it was possible that Hess was suffering from a split mind.
He was imprisoned in England and later stood trial at Nuremburg as a war criminal and imprisoned thereafter in Spandau.

Our Parents Visit – America Comes to Our Aid

"Give us the tools and we will finish the job."
Sir Winston Churchill, February 9, 1941

By the summer of 1941, Britain's army had grown much stronger. There were thirty-four active divisions and five armoured divisions. The Home Guard had been formed and armed. It consisted of civilians who, either through age, exemption or for medical reasons, were not 'called up' for the Forces.

The war in North Africa had progressed well. Bardia was surrounded on January 5, Tobruk was taken a fortnight later. On January 19, the Desert Rats re-occupied Karsala in the Sudan and on the 20th, invaded the Italian colony of Eritrea. On February 6, Benghazi was captured.

However, the German fleet had gained in strength by this time and large-scale attacks on convoys carrying food to Britain were launched. In March, Mr Churchill read a paper to a secret session of the House of Commons which was entitled 'The Battle of the Atlantic' in which he stated:

"The next four months should enable us to defeat the attempt to strangle our food supplies and our connection with the United States. For this purpose we must take the offensive against the U-boat and others wherever we can and whenever we can."

In his book 'The Grand Alliance', Winston Churchill states:

"The U-boats now began to use new methods, which became known as 'wolf-pack' tactics. These consisted of attacks from different directions by several U-boats operating on the surface at full speed unless detected in the approach. Under these conditions only the destroyers could rapidly overhaul them.

These tactics, which formed the keynote of the conflict for the next year or more presented us with two problems: First, how to defend our convoys against this high speed night attack in which the asdic was virtually impotent. The solution lay not only in the multiplication of fast escorts, but still more in the development of effective Radar. The second need was to exploit the vulnerability to air attack of the surfaced U-boat [...]. For this we needed an air weapon which would kill, and also time to train both our sea and air forces in its use. When eventually both these problems were solved, the U-boat was once more driven back to the submerged attack, in which it could be dealt with by the older and well-tried methods."

Once again the United States came to Britain's aid – on March 11, the Lease-Land Bill was passed. Basically to send supplies to Britain where the Battle of the Atlantic was being fought, talks were held in Washington regarding more positive help and American officers were sent to choose bases for naval escorts and air forces. Mr Churchill cabled to President Roosevelt:

"Our blessings from the whole British Empire go out to you and the American nation for this very present help in time of trouble."

Gradually the horrors of the 'Blitz' that I had experienced on my visit to London, faded from my mind so when in the winter of 1941, we had a 'raid' of our own, I found it quite exciting.
The town where we lived offered no tempting target to the enemy bombers as there were no military depots (at that time) nor large aircraft factories nearby. However one night, meeting more opposition perhaps than they had bargained for from the anti-aircraft barrage, a section of the German Luftwaffe decided to jettison a load of incendiary bombs before turning for home.
We awoke to the 'whoosh, whoosh' of something falling from the sky and running to look out the window – being careful to put out the light because of the 'Black-out' (black curtains or frames on which were nailed black material to prevent any light indicating to the enemy above where the towns were) John and I were amazed to see what appeared to be the whole town on fire. Actual damage to property was comparatively slight, but the surprise attack had caught the local Fire Brigade unprepared and several houses and quite a few farm buildings and haystacks were lost.
After this, however, Mr and Mrs Carpenter decided, we must sleep in the Anderson shelter, a large steel construction which was supported on four hefty legs and which was supposed to be strong enough to support the weight of a house if it should collapse. It

served as a dining table during the day and a safe place to sleep at night. Before the erection of this shelter we used to sit in. the cupboard under the stairs on the rare occasions when the air-raid siren sounded the alarm of enemy planes approaching the vicinity. In those days we were reminded constantly not to waste water and every home did its utmost to conserve water in every way possible. Around the bath-tub a black line was painted and when the bath water reached this point the water was four inches deep – the maximum allowed for the Saturday night ablution. It is impossible to forget the torture of sitting shivering in an unheated bathroom surrounded by four inches of water which barely reached one's navel.

On street corners 'static' water tanks were built. These were made of steel and contained thousands of gallons of water for use in the event of the main supply being damaged, in particular for use by the fire brigade. They seemed vast to us children and although playing in or around them was strictly forbidden, few of us could resist the temptation. We sailed our boats in them and even ourselves by means of boats made out of planks which we propelled across from side to side by means or paddling with our hands.

I invented a great game of my own in which I indulged whenever there was no one near the tank. I had obtained a box of 22 bullets from somewhere – I can't remember where – and I had discovered that by removing the bullet head with a pair of pliers and then resealing the cordite in the base, I could fire this missile from a catapult against the wall of the tank. This produced not only a most satisfying 'crack' as it exploded but also a series of underwater echoes like a depth charge.

One Saturday afternoon, it must have been around tea-time for there was no one about, some of my school mates were playing round the tank, climbing up the steep sides, then letting go and jumping to the ground again. It was a bitter afternoon and I huddled into my overcoat which was much too short and beginning to wear thin, and stood watching them. They soon tired of this particular game.

"Let's see if we can walk round the edge," suggested one of the recognised 'leaders' of the form above mine.

"You can't balance on that, the edge is too thin."

"Garn, you're scared!" taunted the other. No one likes to be called a coward and without another word he scrambled up to the top of the tank and pulling himself first into a kneeling position and then very gingerly up to his feet he stood swaying with his arms outstretched like a tight-rope walker.

We waited in terrified fascination as he took one step, then two more. Then with a scream I shall remember all my life he overbalanced and toppled into the icy water.

For a moment no one moved. Finally, the other boys began to scramble up the side of the tank. They hung on to the edge calling to their comrade and trying vainly to grab him as he struggled to get out, finally disappearing out of sight – for he had not been able to swim.

After a few moments I raced down the road in search of help. Round the corner was a shop I knew stayed open late on a Saturday – a little general store, the owner of which I knew quite well. I dashed in and reaching the counter gasped out an incoherent account of what had happened. The owner of the shop and the only customer – who by coincidence happened to be the local police constable – ran out and made full speed to the tank. The policeman went straight up the tank and flinging himself in fully clothed, pulled out the boy in a matter of seconds. It was already too late. The icy water together with the fact – proved later at the inquest – that he had a bad heart had combined to end the life of this unfortunate boy to whom, it seemed incredible to think, I had been talking only the day before. It could have been me – or even John. Once again I had been brought face to face with death, only this time it wasn't some strange soldier who had died on a train or an airman who had disintegrated without trace, it was someone I had known, talked to, laughed with – I grew up a lot that day.

It must have been in the summer of 1942 that my parents came to stay. We were wildly excited for although both John and I had been to visit them in London and then earlier this year had met them at a halfway point for a day, this was going to be something extra special.

Mr and Mrs Carpenter had found them accommodation in the town about half a mile away from our billet in the house of a friend of theirs, and as the day drew near we became more and more excited. At last it arrived.

John and I kept wandering through the house unable to settle to anything until at last in exasperation Mrs Carpenter cried: "Oh, for goodness sake go down to the station now, even if it is nearly an hour before the train – I can't stand your fidgets any longer!"

We needed no second bidding. Dressed in our best school clothes, hair smartly slicked back and shoes highly polished, we hoped our parents would be proud of us.

As luck would have it Mrs Carpenter's father was standing on the platform.

"My my, you look very smart. What's up then?"

"You know, Mother and Father are coming," I cried. He pretended to be surprised.

"Well, are they now – that will be nice for you. I remember when I was a lad..." and he was off on one of his reminiscences. It kept us amused and out of mischief until we heard the distant wail of a steam engine's whistle and after a few moments the longed-for train had arrived.

Once again I was struck by the change in Mother and Father, particularly my father, who seemed now an old man. He looked ill more than usual – and I learned late he'd had a recurrence of his old trouble and in fact hadn't been well since he'd lost everything in the blitz.

John and I accompanied them to the lodgings and helped them settle

It was, on the whole, a very successful visit. The change of scenery and air and the country food – even if scanty – must have done them good.

We made several expeditions to nearby places of interest. Just outside the town was an ancient Roman castle – a man-made hill stepped on all sides. Important archaeological discoveries had been made and here, of course, my father was in his element, surrounded by antiquity. We had several picnics on the grassy slopes while he searched the dips and ditches for pottery shards exposed through the earth's erosion – he even attempted a modest 'dig' of his own, borrowing Mr Carpenter's garden spade, but we found no evidence of previous existence on this windswept desolate mound, apart from a few round pebbles which the locals say were brought there by early-Britains from the coast to use in their slings against the Roman invaders under Julius Caesar.

While Mother and Father were with us we were able to go somewhere we had been eager to explore for a long time – at least I had been keen. John was only interested because he was determined not to be left out.

In the town there was an hotel – I think it was probably an old coaching inn – that was reputed to be unique. It had a Right of Way through the middle of it!

When I told my farther he was as intrigued as I had been and as they served Sunday lunches it was decided that we would all go and have a meal there as an extra special treat.

It was the first time John and I had ever been in an hotel and we found the whole experience very exciting.

The lower part of the building which consisted of bars, the dining-room, and two lounges was in two portions divided by an ordinary alley-way which, although barred to cars, was used as a public thoroughfare by pedestrians, cyclists and even riders on horseback. Above the passage was ceiling by some form of stone, I think, along which a magnificent vine was trained. Upstairs I was told the rooms actually traversed the passage – I could imagine on some occasions the visitors might suffer rather noisy nights!

The dining-room, to which we were solemnly conducted by a tall gentleman in a black suit, was large and elegant. It had wide windows down one side draped with long red velvet curtains, held back with golden cords, and on the floor was a black and red patterned carpet. It seemed the very height of luxury.

The meal was sumptuous by wartime standards. We had soup which really tasted of tomatoes instead of the usual potato water which reminded me of nothing so much as stewed cardboard. Then a delicious pie which mother said was either rabbit or hare but it tasted delicious. This was followed by a mixture of blackberry and apple whipped up with a thin cream – probably off the top of the milk mother commented. We left the table feeling really full for the first time for many weeks. It was a most successful day's outing combining intellectual interest with physical satisfaction!

After Mother and Father returned to London I became more rebellious, much to the despair of both my foster parents and my teachers who had hoped that seeing my parents again would settle me down for a while at least – this was not the case however.

I became involved in a whole series of 'troublesome episodes', as the headmaster – to whom I was constantly presenting myself for punishment – phrased it.

First of all was the case of the 'Apple Scrumping'. About a mile and a half from the school was a large orchard owned by a farmer called Goodbody. He was disliked heartily by most people in the town, particularly so by us schoolboys. Nearly crippled by arthritis he was gnarled and twisted, his bony face with its beady eyes and sunken cheeks emphasising his cadaverousness, he was nicknamed Dogsbody by the inmates of the school.

It was an endless source of entertainment to try to gain access to Dogsbody's orchard – not an easy task for he had surrounded his land with high chain-link fencing surmounted by a double strand of barbed wire. He also kept two very fierce dogs which wandered at will amongst the fruit trees.

One day a friend and I decided to put into action a campaign for invading the orchard that we had been planning for a long while. Armed with a length of rope, some wire cutters, two sacks and some rather revolting bones that I had removed from Mrs Carpenter's dustbin – this, I had heard was what gypsies did when they went stealing – we set off one afternoon after school.

On the end of the rope we had fastened a bent piece of thick galvanised wire, thus making a crude grappling hook. With expertise gained by much practise in the school grounds we soon had this hooked at the top of the wire. Up I scrambled like a commando going over an assault course and at the top laid the sacks over the barbed wire. Sitting gingerly astride I waited for my friend to join me. We surveyed the scene – so far so good. Down the other side we scrambled, the most difficult bit being the removal of the sacks which were needed in phase two of the operation. The rope we left hooked into the fence – very fortunately as it turned out.

Cautiously we proceeded to a section of small heavily laden apple trees which we had previously agreed offered the best yield. Energetically we set to, stripping the trees as quickly as possible of their burden and transferring the fruit to the sacks.

Suddenly, like bats out of hell, with a terrifying snarling the dogs descended upon us. With great presence of mind I remembered to snatch the bag of greasy bones out of my trouser pocket and scattered them in the midst of snapping jaws and whipping tails, and without more ado we flew back to the fence.

Unfortunately our well-laid plans miscarried somewhat. We had filled our sacks with apples and so had no padding for the barbed wire. In the heat of the moment I flung my blazer over to protect our tender parts and as we dropped over the other side I reached up and pulled violently at my coat. With a horrifying rip of tearing cloth it came down but left impaled on the wire was part of the inside facing from the back of the neck – the piece in fact where nine out of ten blazers are marked with the owner's name, and mine was no exception. Luck was definitely against me for the rest of the jacket was intact.

Small consolation that we sold our apples to our school friends for a halfpenny a pound – an expensive transaction for me who received twelve of the best from the headmaster and a week of bed at six o'clock from Mr. Carpenter as punishment.

The next escapade was provoked by another unsympathetic character, Stan Purvis who owned one of the allotments adjoining the school playing fields.

It had become a habit with me to practise football nearly every evening after tea, and we were allowed to play on the strip of land behind the allotments. Separated only by a low wire fence, at least a dozen times in an evening's play, the ball would sail over the fence and land amongst the vegetables. Stan, who always seemed to be there, would return the ball with a grumble or scowl, and on this particular evening, seeming more disagreeable than ever, he informed us angrily that next time he would "put his bloody pitchfork through it!"

Within five minutes the ball landed again in his plot and, sure enough, before returning it to us he deflated the ball, leaving three or four neat holes where he had viciously stabbed it with his fork. This was the end of the game but not of the episode. I was furious – I really wanted to do something violent.

"Let's teach the old b**** a lesson," I said to the others.

"What shall we do?"

"Meet me here after dark - let's say quarter to seven and I'll show you," I said.

I knew it would be difficult to get away from the house and I wondered how many of the others would be able to accomplish it. However at 7 p.m. three of us met as planned and climbed over the low wire into Stew Purvis' allotment. There, working like a team of saboteurs we silently went to work pulling out every vegetable in his plot – carrots, turnips, onions – every living thing. We laid them neatly in rows like dead soldiers before with a great sense of injustice avenged we crept silently home.

Of course we were punished – but I for one would willingly have done the same again. I had done something positive to relieve my bitterness.

HOME GUARD – SEX WAS TABOO

"The war goes on upon many fronts and before it is over there may be yet further fighting that will be developed"
Sir Winston Churchill.

It was now a number of years since I had been adopted by Mr and Mrs Carpenter. I was accustomed to being away from my real mother and father whom I had seen not more than twice a year since I left home, but I never for a moment forgot that this was a temporary existence and that once the war was over I would return to London. During my stay I had not grown to love them as some evacuated children had done, and neither had they become particularly fond of me although, as I have mentioned before they were truly attached to my brother John. I am sure not a week went by without my giving them some worry or other and very little in the way of thanks for their goodness to me. I was now a hard rather bitter boy, introverted, unsociable and rebellious of all discipline. I respected Mrs Carpenter who was a typical hard-working country woman who admired and respected her husband. She deferred to him in everything except household matters which were entirely her department and where she reigned supreme.

Mr Carpenter, however, was a different kettle of fish altogether. He was an unfortunate man in as much as he was not blessed with good looks having a squint in his left eye. Because of this and intermittent ill health he had not been 'called up' and worked for the council as a civil servant – a secure but not very remunerative job. He was sure of a regular salary and the knowledge that unless he did something really bad, he could never be sacked. Because he was in fact a minor government official he was able to run a small car – an Austin – one of the few privileges in these days of austerity. His education had been limited and probably because of this he held very opinionated and bigoted views on most subjects, including life in general. The main causes of conflict between us were his disciplinarian and Victorian views on the upbringing of children – "Children should be seen and not heard" and "Spare the rod and spoil the child" being two of his favourite maxims. I had perforce to learn to live with this outlook but it did not prevent me from many a beating for what I considered very minor offences. He was a man who seemed to have a special interest in the anatomy of the human body for he received weekly a nudist publication, copies of which I had discovered one day when, having nothing better to do, I had entered his private room to have a look round. There were a whole pile of back numbers of these magazines – put there to be out of my reach I suppose – and these were a real revelation to me. I returned, in fact, many times to browse through these, to me utterly disgusting (though fascinating!) books, utterly amazed at the intriguing, photographs of men and women with no clothes on in the most strange positions.

After the discovery of this secret store of 'dirty' books I felt sure that Mr Carpenter as some sort of sex-maniac. Why else would he subscribe to such obscene publications?

For schoolboys, the subject of sex was taboo. We had no education even on the sexual functions of the human body. Our limited knowledge was gained through scraps of information gleaned from our more sophisticated school mates who in most cases anyway had little to do with normal sexual relations. Many of the older boys had discovered the pleasure of masturbation and it was a known fact that some went off to the fields nearby where they would assist one another in the tranquillity of the countryside without fear of being detected.

It had never occurred to me that 'old' people indulged in love-making. I thought it was an activity only partaken by the young. It was a rude awakening therefore and a gross embarrassment to my foster parents when, coming home early from Sunday school because of a bout of earache, I found them in the bedroom in a very compromising position. Hearing their voices I had gone along to report why I had returned. I do not know which of us was the more shocked. It certainly strained relations even more between us for quite a time. It also seemed to me to confirm my suspicion that there was something sexually abnormal about Mr Carpenter – a man of over forty in bed with his wife on a Sunday morning! After this incident it dawned on me why every Sunday, come what may I was packed off to church and Sunday school.

Often I would just go by the church to read the details of the sermon in case I was asked questions about the text, then I would go and spend the collection money on a milkshake and a bun at the local milk bar – one of the few places for social gathering open. Mr Carpenter was a member of the Home Guard. I have stated elsewhere that this was a force of men who were for some reason or another exempt from active service. The commanders were in many cases officers from the First World War who were enthusiastic and professional leaders although their 'men' in many cases left much to be desired, as most of them were either over sixty or had some incapacity. The equipment also was inadequate, most of the rifles being very old and worn. Mr Carpenter was lucky enough to have a fairly new weapon and this he cleaned with loving care several evenings a week, methodically pulling 'four by two' (a piece of flannel 4 inches by 2 inches attached to a cord) through the barrel, and oiling and greasing the mechanism. The chief function of this Home Force was to be prepared to fight alongside the army in the event of an all out invasion of the country.

The winter evenings were long and very dark, no lights being permitted to show from any building, and householders diligently made wooden frames covered in black material to cover every window at night. Wardens patrolled the streets after dark to ensure that there was no violation and their shouts of "Shut that bloody door!" would sometimes break the silence of the night as some neighbour, by opening a door, inadvertently cast a light into the otherwise complete darkness. A total 'Blackout' was enforced at night; persons who had to go out after dark carried a pocket torch which was always pointed downwards, never up, as supposedly its light might be seen by enemy aircraft. There were no street lights of any sort and the few cars which had not been taken by the military had specially dimmed headlights.

More persons were injured by falling at night in the unlit streets than by enemy action, especially elderly people groping their way like the blind as they attended church on Sunday evening.

Although there were several public shelters in the town – steel and concrete buildings reinforced with sandbags against the walls – most people had some form of shelter of their own. Anderson shelters like the Carpenter's inside the house or Morison shelters in the garden. These were corrugated iron constructions which were half sunk in the earth, the soil removed in this operation being banked against the sides and on the top. These also could be reinforced with sandbags. The Morison shelters were horribly damp and cold and must have been very unhealthy to sleep in as many families did.

Most people did 'something to help the war effort' in their spare time. I have mentioned the concentrated growing of vegetables in the 'Dig for Victory' campaign carried out in the gardens and allotments. Most women knitted clothes for 'the boys' for which a special ration of khaki, navy-blue or air force grey wool was issued. Socks, gloves and scarves were the favourites – goodness knows how many ill-fitting garments were received by the long-suffering troops!

Camouflage nets could also be made at home for which the Government paid a nominal amount.

One of the most pleasurable jobs that children could do, and one which I thoroughly enjoyed, was collecting mushrooms when they were in season. These grew in abundance in the nearby fields where cattle grazed – the manure being an essential requirement for mushroom propagation. In order to be sure of a good collection one had to be up very early, and to rise about half-past five and venture forth into the new misty September morning and walk through the dewy fields was quite magical. The dew would hang on the myriad of little spider webs making 'fairy gossamer'. It was with a never failing sense of excitement that I searched the wet grass for the white domes. When the basket was full I had to hold out the front of my coat or cape in order to accommodate them. Once back home it was tantalizing to smell them sizzling in the pan in the meagre bacon fat left over from the day before and to know that for once breakfast would be a really satisfying meal.

Another activity open to schoolboys was the OTC (Officers' Training Corps), which prepared them for the army at seventeen years of age. A junior branch called the JTC (Junior Training Corps) was created later so that boys from the age of twelve upwards could receive some form of military training. At first uniforms were hard to come by and the cadets looked an odd collection with hats too big and trousers too short and blouses too tight, but eventually they were all kitted out quite respectably and looked very smart on their weekly parades.

The Corp as it was known was officiated over by Waxey who was in his element, of course, bawling at everyone in his raucous sergeant-major's voice. Each school corp was affiliated to a regiment of the British Army and wore the appropriate badge in its cap or beret. On the shoulder a flash indicated from which school the corp came. The uniform consisted of battle-dress blouse, khaki trousers, puttees (which were a devil to put on) boots and beret or peak cap if one was a member of the band. Because of my interest in music and my progress with the town band I decided to join the Corp, although basically I was not keen on the military aspect of parades, drilling and general 'togetherness' of Corp life.

Probably because a number of boys from our school were in the local band, the Corp band was of a very high standard. The Drum Major was a senior who was a good drummer and bugler and he had authority and 'presence'. We obtained most of our instruments from the regiment to whom we were affiliated, most of whom were serving abroad so presumably didn't need their full quota.

I must admit that I quite enjoyed going on weekend camps. It got me out of the Carpenters' house and there was something rather exciting about night manoeuvres.

In the holidays we could go on courses if we liked, the most popular being the 'weapons' course and the 'wireless' course.

In the school grounds we built an assault course consisting of simulated parachute jumps – a long wire reaching from the top of a

very high tree down to the ground at an angle down which one slid on
a pulley at great speed. Another rope from which we were required to swing across a pool of very dirty water – a great source of entertainment this, for several boys never made it across and subsequently ended up in the slimy stagnant evil-smelling sludge. There was a tunnel through which we had to crawl in full gear; and a high vertical wall to scale. We also had on the premises a rifle range where we were allowed to shoot .22 rifles, and an armoury where there were Bren guns, Sten guns and an old Lewis gun (none of which had firing pins so were quite safe) which we learned to strip down and put together again after oiling and greasing.

Any cadet over the age of sixteen was automatically attached to the local Home Guard in preparation for a possible invasion and several manoeuvres were held while I was a junior, where our boys usually took the part of the enemy in a planned campaign. Although an invasion was still a possibility events had moved dramatically in other directions during 1941/42.

On August 9, 1941, the historic meeting between Winston Churchill and President Roosevelt had taken place at Placentia Bay in Newfoundland. This meeting was decided upon because of growing concern in the two countries about the increasing menace from Japan. They had occupied Indo-China which meant they were in a position to attack the British in Malaya, the Dutch in the East Indies, and the American bases in the Philippine Islands.

President Roosevelt asked the Japanese government to neutralize Indo-China and withdraw their troops and at the same time he ordered Japanese assets in the U.S. to be frozen which brought trade between the two countries to a standstill.

A little later the British and Dutch followed suit, the move from the latter meant that Japan was deprived of her oil supply.

The Atlantic Charter was drawn up as a result of the meeting between the two leaders at Placentia in which the American Lease-Lend agreement was increased enormously.

During this period also, Hitler invaded the Soviet Union, and so Russia joined 'The Allies' and their struggle for survival.

Winston Churchill summed up British priorities as follows:

First: the defence of Britain including the threat of invasion and the U-boat war.
Second: the struggle in the Middle East and Mediterranean where intense fighting was still going on.
Third: supplies to the new ally, Russia.
Fourth: resistance to the Japanese assault.

In 1939, Japan were still fighting a war with China begun in 1937, and were also wrangling with Russia about boundaries between Manchukuo and Outer Mongolia. British support and sympathy lay with China so relations with Japan were not very friendly. When France fell and the possibility of invasion of Britain by Germany in 1940, Japan felt she might gain something. The Army Minister,

General Hata, withdrew from the Cabinet, and Admiral Yonai resigned as Prime Minister. The new Prime Minister was Prince Konoye, who negotiated the Tripartite Pact with Germany and Italy. This meant that if America entered the war as Britain's ally, Japan would join the Axis.

In 1941, Britain, Holland, and the United States enforced embargoes on Japan, cutting off supplies of oil on which the Navy depended. The Japanese Navy was forced to live on its oil reserves which were soon greatly depleted, and it was obvious that Japan would have to reach an agreement with America or go to war. The United States demanded Japanese withdrawal from Indo-China and China.

In October Prince Konoye resigned, and General Tojo became Prime Minister. He renewed diplomatic negotiations with United States and after talks with American representatives, reported to the Emperor that it might be necessary to go to war.

On November 1, 1941, General Chiang Kai-Shek warned Britain and America that in his opinion the Japanese were about to attack Kunming from Indo-China and cut the Burma Road. He asked for British air assistance and American aid to defend Yunnan, for he felt it was possible that if the Japanese broke the Chinese front, the British air and sea co-ordination with the United States and the Dutch East Indies would be affected.

Britain felt it was vital to support Chiang Kai-Shek for the cutting of the Burma Road by Japan would leave them with large forces to attack north and south.

Churchill asked Roosevelt to warn Japan against such a move, but Roosevelt replied that he didn't think the situation was as grave as Churchill considered, and that "Any new formalised verbal warning or remonstrance, might ... have an even chance of producing the opposite effect ... the whole problem will have our continuing and earnest attention, study and effort."

He also stated he would increase Lease-Lend to China, and build up the American Volunteer Air Force there.

Eventually Japan agreed to evacuate Indo-China if U.S. would supply her with petroleum. This did nothing to help Chiang Kai-Shek and China however and the U.S. drew up instead a 'Ten Point Proposal', the most important clauses of which stated:

"The Government of Japan will withdraw all military, naval, air and police forces from China and Indo-China
The Government of the United States and the Government of Japan will not support – militarily, politically, or economically – any Government or regime in China other than the National Government of the Republic of China with capital temporarily at Chungking."

On November 26, 1941, President Roosevelt sent a message to the High Commissioner of the Philippines which said:

"Preparations are becoming apparent ... for an early aggressive movement of some character, although as to strength or whether it

will be directed against the Burma Road, Thailand, Malay Peninsula, Netherlands, East Indies or the Philippines. Advance against Thailand seems the most probable. I consider it possible that this next Japanese aggression might cause an outbreak of hostilities between U.S. and Japan."

About this time, America succeeded in breaking the Japanese cipher and therefore was able to decode their military and diplomatic messages and telegrams. On November 30, a message from Tokyo to Berlin to the Japanese Ambassador advising him to inform Hitler and Ribbentrop that:

"... There is extreme danger that war may suddenly break out between the Anglo-Saxon nations and Japan through some clash of arms, and add that the time of the breaking out of this war may come quicker than anyone dreams."

On December 7, 1941, Japanese bombers roared out of the sky and attacked the American Fleet at Pearl Harbour.
The United States was at war!

THE YANKS ARRIVE – TOOTSIE ROLLS & CHEWING GUM

The United States has been attacked and become at war with the three Axis Powers.
Sir Winston Churchill, 10 January, 1942.

I have said there were no military installations anywhere near the town, but in fact there was an army camp about three miles away. Situated on rising ground it had only one approach road – a narrow lane lined with high hawthorn hedges which were covered with sharp thorns and masses of red berries. This camp consisted of lines of brown wooden huts, evenly spaced, each one built up on stilts about three feet off the ground. It had been deserted since I arrived in the vicinity, and I had gone there several times to explore, for the security fence had many gaps through which one could crawl to gain access.

It must have been some time in 1943 that this deserted camp became occupied again and this time by American troops. They had arrived, we learned, from North Africa, and were soldiers of one of the finest U.S. infantry divisions; they had been used both in the invasion of North Africa and in the Sicily landing (which had resulted in the capitulation of the Italian Army). They were men of the First Division and, although at the time it was not generally known, these veterans of war were to be used to spearhead the invasion on 'D' Day with landings on the French coast off Normandy.

The arrival of the U.S. troops in the area was the beginning of a new life and another world for me – a schoolboy into the world of men. In the next twelve months I was to see and hear things which I could never dream existed. I was to see men drunk, men gambling and frequently, men fighting and on one occasion to see a man killed with a knife in front of my eyes. I was to hear the foulest barrack-room language and to learn about women and how easily they succumbed to amorous advances. I was to meet soldiers who were mentally and sexually perverted.

During this year also I was to remember many acts of true kindness by soldiers, many at whom were only a ten years older than myself who just wanted to talk to and be with anyone not wearing khaki. The G.I.'s were always friendly and eager to talk to us children – after being in foreign parts, I suppose, being able to speak English made them feel more at home.

Within a few days of their arrival, the G.I.'s were being followed in the streets by flocks of children crying: "Got any gum, chum?" Chewing-gum was a novelty they had introduced into England from the New World. Our meagre ration of sweets per week was supplemented, by the candy we could scrounge from the soldiers. Once a week was P.X. day when they drew their allowance of candy, gum and cigarettes. On this day hordes of children would hang around the camp knowing full well that some of the men would draw their ration and give it all away. For our persistency we were rewarded with 'Hershey Chocolate Bars', 'Life Savers', and 'Tootsie Rolls'. On some occasions we had more candy than we could eat and any excess sweets could be bartered at school and with friends for army badges and the like.

Getting into the camp, either at weekends in daylight or in the dark of evening presented no great problem for we soon got to know the guard on the main gate and walked straight through, or else we made up some story that we were on some errand for Sergeant So-and-So and nine times out of ten we got away with it. If for any reason these ways proved impractical there was always the alternative of the broken barbed wire fence near the railway line under which we could crawl. I was caught doing just this on more than one occasion and it is a wonder I was never shot at by some trigger-happy guard! After getting into the camp grounds it was often quite a feat to find which hut we were looking for. This was the most dangerous time, getting in and out of the camp especially on nights when there was no moon – wandering around looking for a familiar face inside the huts whose doors we tried in turn.

I was spending more and more of my leisure time at the camp where, like a gambler unable to control his passion, I headed for the company of the G.I's at weekends and whenever I could escape in the evenings. It was there that I could be sure of a welcome, warmth and interest – not to mention the many gifts that were thrust upon me by the over-generous friends that I had made. In the comfort of one of the huts I would sit listening to the tales and stories or their homes in America – of the wide open spaces, the luxury and of their families and children. It all sounded so wonderful and I had no reason to disbelieve that everyone in

America was a millionaire and lived in a skyscraper. I was shown pictures of their wives, families and girlfriends in their billfolds, and listened wide-eyed as they told me of life in the United States. Seeing the way they lived in the Services, which seemed to me sheer luxury, I had no reason to think they were either lying or exaggerating.

I don't recall seeing many black G.I.'s and, if I did, we spent no time in their company but I do remember the many lectures I received, especially from one soldier, telling me how bad 'niggers' were. It was a lengthy one-sided discussion telling me everything that was wrong with blacks, of how they were naturally lazy, stole and raped white women and that the way they dealt with them 'where he was from' was to nail their balls to the wooden floor of a deserted house and set fire to the house. Many black G.I.'s passed through the town, later in convoys to go across the Channel to fight in Europe, but at this time I do not think black and white troops were integrated and I don't remember ever speaking to one after what I had been told. It was a very biased introduction to a major American problem and I think I can be forgiven for the fact that it was a long time before I could even think about the problem objectively.

I was soon to find out that my secret way through the barbed wire by the railway line was also used by others. It was the quietest part of the perimeter where sentries ambled by only once or twice an hour. Through the wire and over railroad track led to town and many G.I.'s used this way to get out at nights when no town passes were issued.

One day on conker* collecting expedition some few hundred yards from the camp perimeter, I saw for the first time in my life something most strange and so intriguing that I returned on a number at other occasions to further my education. A number of young girls – and some not so young – all in colourful summer dresses were standing near the railway tracks in a field. They seemed to be doing nothing in particular just waiting. Some were standing alone, others were in pairs talking. It was not long before my curiosity was rewarded.

Coming through my secret exit from the camp under the barbed wire, there appeared a G. I. who walked up to one of the girls in the field, and after a brief tête à tête disappeared into the long grass; in a very short time he reappeared and returned to camp the way he had come. Within a matter of half an hour, four or five other soldiers followed the same routine, none of them spending more than five minutes with any girl.

These pretty girls standing outside the camp became a familiar sight in the next few weeks and gave me further occasion to

---

* 'Conkers' or horse chestnuts were used in a popular game whereby one strung the nut on a piece of string and used it in the manner of an old-time knight's 'morning star'. If you demolished your opponent's conker yours became a 'oner', if victorious again it was a 'twicer' and so on <u>ad. inf.</u>

investigate and it was soon quite obvious even at my tender age and limited knowledge, what was going on.

With other boys from school I would go for a 'peep-show' to watch these strange goings on. Concealed either in the long grass or in nearby trees we would watch for hours in fascination as the couples copulated.

This fraternization went on for weeks until at last the authorities discovered what was happening and put a stop to it, by which time the field was scattered with evidence of love-making on a massive scale. At the time I seem to remember the tariff was five shillings to make the acquaintance of one of these girls who would be ready, willing and waiting regardless of the weather.

On some evenings the soldiers were given passes to go into town but there was very little to do. The restaurants were closed and in many cases G.I.'s were not welcome in the pubs where, although beer was not rationed, it was in short supply and kept for the 'locals' who resented outside intrusion.

On rare occasions dances were organised on Saturday nights, but since the arrival of the Americans they had caused trouble between the G.I.'s and the local youths and members of the British Army visiting the town. Several times quite vicious fights had broken out, although it was difficult to understand what they had to fight about considering they were allies fighting a common enemy. Provocation was the cause of much of the trouble and friction together with utter boredom. Such remarks as "bloody Yanks", together with accusations that they had only come into the war after America was attacked at Pearl Harbour were sufficient to start a riot on a Saturday night. There was also no doubt, a certain amount of jealousy on the part of the British boys in their ill-fitting, rough uniforms, whenever they met up with the G.I.'s who had more money and more of everything. One of the more polite sayings of the time when referring to our American allies was: "They're over-paid, over-sexed, and over here."

On evenings when they were allowed out of camp, there was literally nothing to do and they roamed the streets in packs, looking for some form of amusement. The town was deserted with few people on the streets – houses unlit and unfriendly – and the town patrolled by M.P's waiting to carry off any soldier who had been lucky enough to find a few shots of whisky. The chances of finding any female company were as likely as finding a snowball in hell: many would return disillusioned to camp early in the evening where at least it was warm and there was always something going on. Some did return with amazing stories of their evening's activities together with the most intimate details of their sexual conquests, which in most cases, I think, were imaginary. On one evening, however, I do recall a young G.I. returning with some such story and, after relating every detail to his disbelieving buddies, he produced from his pocket evidence that he had presumably deflowered a virgin by proudly hanging a blood-stained rubber over his bunk for all in the hut to see a trophy of his evening's conquest.

Boredom was one of the worst enemies for the G.I.'s; there was little or nothing to amuse them in the evenings when they were confined to camp, and even less to do in town when they were allowed the occasional pass. From time to time professional entertainment came to the camp in the way of well-known personalities from America. Some of the top artists and musicians spent months touring the bases in England entertaining the boys. On one such visit a group of musicians led by the incredible Gene Kruper appeared.

On the evening of the performance every soldier in camp, apart from the few in the camp jail, attended – from the General down to the lowliest private and one or two intruders, like myself, who were smuggled into the mess-hall which was packed to capacity. They were sitting on the floor, climbing up into the rafters just to get a glimpse of some of these gorgeous long-legged all-American girls who were in the show. For some of them this was the first contact with the U.S. they had had for a number of years. These camp shows did wonders for their morale but, at the same time, made them very homesick for everything that was American. It was a fantastic performance where the musicians gave their all. The finale was an unbelievable drum solo by the Master himself, which went on for a number of minutes and was greeted with almost hysterical applause by every soldier in the overcrowded hall – a thunderous ovation of whistling, shouting, and. clapping which was deafening. Caps were thrown in the air and the tramping of thousands of pairs of army boots on the wooden floorboards rocked the entire building.

This visit by Gene Kruper to the camp had been a very special event; professional entertainment was a very rare thing and, by contrast, much of the self-made musical entertainment in the evenings was anything but professional. Most evenings music of some sort was being thumped out by a guitarist or two and maybe a mandolin, as two or three of the boys amused their buddies hour after hour with the music they liked. The atmosphere would be thick with smoke as they crowded around the group at one end of the hut. Some sat cross-legged on the floor, others sat on their bunks in various stages of undress or stretched out almost mesmerized, staring up at the fleshy pin-ups on the walls as the monotonous thump, thump, thump of the music went on. For the few of them who disliked Western music or who wanted to sit and read, there was no escape from it; most of them knew all the melodies and all the words and would join in the choruses to add to the bedlam.

By now I had my favourite hut where I was well-known and well-treated. Entering it at any time was like coming home, always toasty warm and always someone to take notice of me and talk to me. It was not necessary to read their names on the metal dog-tags which hung around their necks; I knew them all by their first names and they knew mine. I had literally been adopted by them. P.X. day became almost an embarrassment when I would be showered with chocolate, chewing-gum and candy of every sort.

Even quantities of cigarettes, which were almost unobtainable were given to me to take home to my 'father'. These never did arrive but, instead, fetched a good price on the black market! Some days I had to take a school friend along just to help me home with all the contraband which I had been given.

In exchange for these kindnesses I ran errands for my G.I. buddies, especially when they were confined to barracks. Most nights they had early curfew which meant no one outside the camp after 9 p.m. On these evenings there were dozens of jobs I could do for them – from buying and delivering flowers to their girlfriends in town to the most common errand of getting them something to eat. Their last mess meal was at 6 p.m., so by 9 or 10 o'clock, anything in the way of food was welcome. Money was no object and if I could find in town, cheese sandwiches, meat pies, sausage rolls or fish and chips, I was always assured of a ready market – with the money in advance.

Fish and chips was the favourite, and also on sale most evenings in town. This traditional English delicacy they all loved; served in newspaper which was the only paper we had and which seemed to improve the flavour with vinegar and salt, it was possibly not very hygienic but I never ever had a complaint from my customers. In an evening I would take orders of up to thirty or forty portions of fish and chips, each order costing one shilling, that was sixpence for the fish which was usually cod, and sixpenny worth of chips. With cash in advance, I would leave the comfort of the barrack room and go out into the unfriendly night and head for the perimeter wire. It was only when there was no moon that it was very difficult to find the whole in the fence, sometimes I went running up and down the enclosure at night like a fenced-in chicken trying to find a way out! After being forbidden entrance one evening with a load of fish and chips, by the guard at the main entrance, I never did use the main gate again, always preferring to use the 'back door' into camp.

The distance down town to Charlie's greasy fish shop was a couple of miles through deserted streets. Using my bike, which had been left in a ditch outside the base, I cycled there in minutes, where I would proudly place my order for thirty or forty bundles to 'take out'. Payment was made in advance and the money I carried in a handkerchief for safety. This collection of heavy silver coins and copper pennies weighing a number of pounds, I would produce from this well-used handkerchief and empty onto the high counter and wait while Charlie made neat little piles, carefully checking that the amount was correct.

Tins of coarse salt and bottles of vinegar were on the tables for the use of customers and, before going out, I would undo each steaming bundle and add a generous helping of both. The journey back took considerably longer as I awkwardly staggered, balancing a large card-board box on the saddle and the handlebars of my bike. It was too heavy and too awkward to ride with this heavy box so I pushed the load for two miles, a strenuous task, especially as much of it was uphill.

My reception back at camp was like the return of Caesar – maybe because those who did not know me might well have thought that I would abscond with the money they had given me. The music would stop as hungry G.I.'s grabbed the bundles, still hot, from the box. By now, after the journey, much of the fat from the fish had soaked through the newspaper covering, as they sat around on bunks, silently munching chunks of fish and licking their greasy fingers.

For this excursion I was handsomely rewarded and often I went and shopped for their evening meal several times a week.

ATTACKED BY A G.I. – BARRACK ROOM FIGHTS

There is a brotherhood in arms between us and our friends of the United States.
Sir Winston Churchill, 1943.

By now I had been installed for a number of months, enjoying the many advantages of knowing my way around the camp. Hundreds of men knew me by sight, if not by name, and I knew sergeants, captains and colonels as well as scores of 'other ranks' but out of respect I only called soldiers below the rank of sergeant by their first name.

At 'chow' time I would borrow a mess-can and march with the boys to the Mess Hall for lunch or dinner as the case may have been. Joining the G.I.'s from 'K' hut, they would put me in the middle file where I was small enough not to be seen by the guards or the eyes of passing officers and I would generally reach the hall undetected. Once I lined up with the men shuffling up to the long heated counter's where their everyday food was better, it seemed to me than our Christmas dinner. Great mounds of fried chicken served with sweet corn which I had never had before the Americans' arrival and which I had grown to love, mountains of creamy-mashed potatoes and crusty brown apple pie which was all washed down with giant size mug of coffee.

Sometimes I went up for two or three helpings of this magnificent food which I thought fit for a king and could never understand why some of the boys complained about it. For me it was sheer heaven as I wandered round with my mess tin heaped with food, looking for a couple of square inches on one of the crowded wooden tables where I could squeeze in, sit down and tuck into my meal. Once in a while I was thrown out by an over-efficient mess sergeant but usually the full support of 'buddies' persuaded them to let me stay. A chorus of G.I.'s calling the sergeant all the bastards under the sun for trying to throw me out, was usually sufficient for me to get a reprieve and most often I was allowed to finish my meal before leaving. Before returning the mess-can and irons to their owner, I lined up like any enlisted man to dunk and sterilize them in vats of scalding water which were provided at the exits.

By now I was almost an expert on the United States of America, having spent many months listening to stories about their lives, families, and occupations back home. I had heard about their big cars, the skyscrapers and the film industry and I could name every State in the Union. It seemed to be the only place worth living in and it was now my dream and ambition to visit this country which, if all I'd heard was true, was bigger and better than anything I could possibly imagine.

The sergeant of 'K' hut – by whom I had been adopted – promised me that when the war was over he would invite me to his home. One of the frequent demands I got was for clothing coupons. No article of clothing could be bought without them and although the G.I.'s had none, they had money and by devious methods I could usually get some from somewhere. Many of the boys wanted them so they could buy leather gloves which were much smarter than the cumbersome woollen gloves issued by Uncle Sam. They also liked to buy scarves for their English girlfriends. In return for my services to the G.I.'s, I received a varied collection of gifts. Army badges, pocket knives, military caps and ball-point pens, which we had never seen in Wartime Europe were all part of the loot which I received and never had to ask for. It could partly have been the lack of understanding of the complicated English money, with its pennies, half-crowns, etc., but their generosity proved to be almost more than I could handle.

The evening business had literally snowballed without me even trying and the result was that I was earning a number of pounds a week with few ways of spending it. I was now in a position to visit two movies on a Saturday, regardless of what was showing. I would attend one cinema at 2 p.m., and at the conclusion, run a mile to the other movie house to catch the 4 o'clock film, where in luxury, I sat through the show like a millionaire, chewing toffee-apples and eating ice-cream. With my earnings I also bought accessories for my bike, which now looked like a Christmas tree and was fitted with a large saddlebag, two-tone bell, a speedometer and two very impressive-looking chrome lamps.

I also sampled a varied selection from their emergency rations. A tin of 'C' ration was not a favourite for, apart from the few pieces of candy, it contained three or four very hard biscuits which tasted like dog biscuits, and we usually threw them away, after removing the sweets from the tin. The 'K' ration came in a rectangular wax-covered box and it was a varied selection, which included a tin of meat and a number of cigarettes. Most sought-after was the 'D' emergency which was a solid slab of hard chocolate, in a sealed box. Sometimes it was badly discoloured – either from age or from bad storage – but still tasted good. At some stage I was given a bag of chocolate powder by one of the boys, which was a great treat and I can remember my amazement at seeing for the first time, the spelling on the packet which read: "Distributed thru the American Red Cross," instead of the normal English spelling 'through'.

One of the few unpleasant G.I.'s I met was Private Symonds who became a problem which I did not know how to handle. He was a small greasy-haired man with a spotty rather 'foxy' face. I had noticed him watching me on several occasions and one day as I was about to leave the camp by the 'back door', hearing a noise behind me I looked around. Private Symonds was following me. I hesitated, wondering what he wanted. I soon found out! He came right up close to me, an intense, devouring look on his face. He seemed to be breathing hard. Before I realised what he was doing he had undone my flies and roughly pulling down my trousers and underpants he started fondling my genitals.

This was the first time anything like this had ever happened to me and I didn't know what to do. I knew the boys at school touched each other when they went off together down to the fields and I knew it gave them some satisfaction, but I had never been involved, although some of the senior boys had on one or two occasions asked me quite politely if I would like to 'come down to the fields' with them, which I had refused just as politely.

But this was horrible! With a strength I didn't know I possessed I managed to push him away and kicking off the clothing clinging round my ankles I swept them up in my arms and ran like a hare away to the fence under which I scrambled as if all the demons in hell were after me. I must have looked a comic sight with my bare bottom looking like a rabbit's scut!

There was only one person I could confide in and whose help I could seek in this matter and that was my friend the sergeant of 'K' hut, and this I did the next time I visited the camp. I don't know what he said to Symonds but I was not bothered again for quite a time, then a similar incident occurred only this time there were others present.

I happened to be standing alone in a corner of 'K' hut reading an American 'comic' paper when suddenly I felt a pinch on my bottom. I jumped round and there was Private Symonds smirking at me.

"Hi Pete, cut that out, you fruit!" shouted one voice.

"Leave the kid's arse alone – you'd rather have the backside of a man than the front of a woman!" was another bawdy remark the result of which was that Symonds slunk away and I was bothered no more. That was not the end of the incident however. The boys took great exception to the Private's persecution of me – no doubt because of my extreme youth, but also because he had been in trouble for the same sort of thing with young boys of the town.

They decided to plan an evening of entertainment for the boys which would also be a lesson to their homosexual buddy to keep his hidden desires hidden in future.

It was a typical evening when everyone was confined to base. The hours dragged after an early 'chow' and the usual activities were going on in the hut. The musicians were, as on most evenings, huddled in a group bashing away at their guitars – the same monotonous rhythm which we all knew so well and the same familiar melodies which were repeated night after night, week after week. Other G.I.'s were writing letters to wives and families, some reading paperbacks, and in one corner a tense game of black-jack was going on.

It was very hot up each end of the room where pot-bellied iron stoves stood. The soldiers in the beds near these fires must sometimes have been nearly roasted alive, and it so happened that Private Symonds had his bed in one of these hot spots. On this particular evening he was engrossed in a paperback thriller that he had drawn that day from the P.X. Every so often he would discard an item of clothing without taking his eyes from the book. First his tie, then his sweater then the top buttons of his shirt were undone. He didn't notice the approach of several G.I.'s who were advancing purposefully towards him.

"Symonds, we're goin' ter teach yer a lesson," said one of the boys who seemed to be the leader. He was also one of the biggest and beefiest and he spoke with a distinct southern drawl.

"We all know that you like goosin' around so we gotta special treat for y'al…"

"Yeah," another large powerfully-muscled Private joined in. "We guess you'd like a little help undressin' as you seem to be so hot – what about those pants you're always in a hurry to get off?"

By now most of the boys had gathered round, some standing, others climbing onto the nearby bunks to get a good view of the 'fun'. Any form of entertainment was welcome for it broke the boredom and tonight looked as if it was going to be something special. Private Symonds waited, looking like a frightened rabbit not knowing where to run to get away. He had not long to wait for as they got near four of the boys grabbed him from his sitting position and with a combined jerk pulled him to his feet.

They carried him from his bunk like a writhing octopus and flung him down in the centre of the floor. Deftly his khaki trousers then his long woollen underpants were removed. Two of the heftiest G.I.'s were sitting on him so he was helpless.

The boys crowded round, cheering and jeering like a crowd at a bullfight waiting for the kill. Suddenly someone produced a can of boot-blacking and a brush and this was handed round from man to man so that each could 'have a go'. With great delight and exemplary assiduousness they worked the black treacly mess into his lower regions – over the cheeks of his bottom and in between as well. All round his genitals - paying particular attention to the penis –until at last every drop was used up.

"I always wanted my own Nigger!" shouted one of the 'helpers'.

Private Symonds barely had the energy to get up from the floor after his ordeal and he crawled back to his bunk wincing with every step for his treatment had been not only degrading but rough and painful as well.

The group of G.I.'s slowly dispersed and the men wandered back to continue their previous occupations. Within minutes the card game was in full swing again and the wail of Western music once more echoed through the hut. Except for the huddled form with the black trunk on the bed by the stove you would not have known anything out of the ordinary had happened.

By the end of each month poverty broke out at camp as the boys counted the days until pay-day. No money for cigarettes, drink or dates, and never a game of crap as no one had sufficient funds to start a game. On pay-day the atmosphere changed to one of excitement and abundance, with them throwing their money around as if it was going out of fashion, and there were always those who had debts to pay back to their buddies and were broke again within twenty-four hours.

By evening card games would be in progress and a crap game would be organised. Gathered at the far end of the hut it would go on for hours – the dices being bounced against the wooden skirting-board. Surrounded by the non-players, who would shout obscene and customary words of encouragement, the dice-players would work themselves into a frenzy, continuing throughout the evening until 'lights-out'. At times there would be a mountain of crumpled dollar bills on the floor which the winner would scoop into his arms and carry off to his bunk to count his winnings. They seemed to have an utter disregard for money. Unbelievable amounts would change hands in an evening, running into thousands of dollars. Maybe they were right. No one was to know but, within weeks, dozens of these youngsters were to die on the Normandy beaches. As was inevitable, there were frequent accusations of cheating. Losers would pathetically go from bunk to bunk trying to borrow money to get back into the game, certain that their lucky break was just about to come. Others who had lost money would go and sit in silence, pouting like children just given a spanking. After some of these games, fights would often break out usually because someone thought they had been cheated, resulting in magnificent fist-fights the like of which I had only ever seen in the movies. I was amazed how, with one punch from a fist, a man could be knocked to the ground with what seemed to be very little effort. Most times the barrack room brawl, were quickly broken up by the N.C.O.'s or by the other G.I.'s a but on one occasion, a man was knifed and killed before someone could intervene.

As usual there had been an accusation that someone had cheated at cards, so two of the boys started to tear one another apart. Clawing, kicking and punching like wild animals within minutes they were both a bloody mess, their noses bleeding. Scratched and bruised, they screamed abuse at one another until, finally separated, both exhausted and panting heavily, the tournament appeared to be over to the disappointment of the onlookers who enjoyed watching the blood-bath. The man who had come off the worst was being cleaned up by his buddies who with towels and a mug full of water were bathing his wounds and attending to one eye which had been badly cut open and was now starting to close up. The hut was suddenly quiet having changed from a madhouse to an almost church-like silence in seconds.

Leaving his bed, the loser, looking more respectable and less bloody than a few minutes before, walked towards his opponent - at stocky man with a slight paunch who was on the other side off the hut. He was leaning against a bedpost smoking a cigarette and still looking dazed from the evening's fight – little did he know that it was to be the last cigarette he would ever smoke. Turning slowly he faced the loser who was now some paces away walking slowly towards him both hands open. With no warning his right hand came forward with an upward movement, striking the G.I. squarely in the stomach. A knife, which must have been hidden in his shirt sleeve was now embedded in the fat man's stomach up to the hilt and the blood came spurting out. Gripping his middle with both hands, his half-smoked cigarette dropped from his lips as he uttered a choked sound as if about to vomit, before he crumpled to the floor.

I watched, horrified. I could hardly believe that this man, who a few moments before had been so very much alive was now dead. The G.I.'s crowded round, hiding the body from my sight, and a particular friend of mine, Private McGooley, came and put his arm round my shoulders.

"Come on, Buddy - I think you should go home, yeah?" and he led me gently through the door. I gave a backward glance and saw they had wrapped the body in a blanket. Really it was all over so quickly I could hardly believe it had happened.

It was only afterwards at home that the reaction set in and I was violently sick. I didn't tell Mrs Carpenter what had made me ill – I was afraid I would be forbidden to go to the camp again and this was unthinkable for by now it had become a regular routine for me to go up there every evening and at weekends. Of course my schoolwork suffered badly for I skimped my homework and private study, but the extra rations released for Mr and Mrs Carpenter by my absence made them quite pleased for me to follow my inclinations in this respect.

By the spring of 1944 there were rumours going round that the American contingent would be moving out. This was the moment they had been training for over the past months. It was common knowledge that soon the Allies were to open a second front but where and when no one knew. An air of depression settled over the camp. These veterans who had been involved in fighting before knew the percentage of casualties in any spearhead landing was very high and they knew that many of them would not see their native land again. They were edgy and not the care-free comrades we had known up to now. Speculation was high that the eventual landing would be in France but some opinions were that it might be Denmark.

One thing was certain, they were highly trained assault troops and when the day came they would be in there first - wherever the battle was.

Daily cases of desertion were reported and much to the disgust of his buddies one of the men from 'K' hut went 'over the hill' – no doubt he considered a few years behind bars a preferable alternative to ending up in a military cemetery in Europe.

D-Day Arrives – A Quick Get-Away

We are waiting for the long-promised invasion – so are the fishes!
Sir Winston Churchill.

Ever since she had entered the war America had been pressing Britain to invade German-occupied France but the great stumbling block to this plan was the absence of good harbours on the Normandy coast. Vice Admiral Lord Louis Mountbatten, who was chief of combined operations set out to solve the problem with the aid of his very able staff. Eventually they hit upon the brilliant plan of building synthetic 'harbours'. These would be created by block ships self-powered to the required position, then sunk to form a breakwater which would provide a large area of sheltered water. Into the sheltered area large floating piers were towed and securely moored at the landward end. These protruded into the sea, thus forming the means for the unloading of men and equipment by coasters and landing craft. These synthetic harbours were known as 'Mulberries'.

Another brilliant idea executed in order to facilitate the Invasion was the invention of PLUTO (pipe line under the ocean) which was laid from the Isle of Wight to Calais to supply fuel for the army vehicles. The forthcoming invasion was given the name 'Overlord', and planned to take place in June. General Eisenhower was appointed to the supreme command and General Montgomery became the commander of the expeditionary forces.

One of the most difficult preparations for D-Day was deceiving the enemy into believing the Invasion was going to be launched across the straits of Dover. Troops were massed in Kent and Sussex and dummy ships were collected at the Cinque Ports and air reconnaissance of the 'wrong' places were carried out.

June 6, was chosen as D-Day as at that time the moon and tides were most favourable. The assault started by three airborne Divisions consisting of one thousand planes and gliders dropping paratroops on the continent at 5 a.m. London time. Then one thousand Royal Air Force and one thousand and four hundred U.S. bombers attacked enemy installations. The first assault troops landed at 6.30 a.m. on beaches along a line Carentan-Bayeaux-Caen. With the Americans on the West, the British and Canadian on the East, the total allied strength available was 2,876,439 men, including seventeen British Divisions of which three were Canadian; twenty U.S. Divisions; one French and one Polish.

In the late evening of June 5, 1944, we were woken by the noise of troop convoys through the town. Every man, woman and child flocked into the streets and hung from the windows to witness this, the beginning of the biggest invasion the world had ever known. An endless stream of trucks filled to capacity with G.I.s in full battle order, rumbled through town, moving south to drive the eight miles to the coast where invasion barges were waiting to take them across the English Channel to war. For the past few days the camp had been under curfew, and no one had been allowed anywhere near it. Now the main gates had been opened for the last time and thousands of trucks passed through, their brilliant headlights turning the night into day as they passed the house at the rate of one every second. The G.I.'s waved to the crowds in the streets who were cheering each truck as it passed, their shouts and good luck wishes drowned by the noise of the engines.

Few went to bed that night but sat and watched from their windows as the continuous stream of vehicles, belching exhaust fumes and producing enough noise to waken the dead passed by. Watching these soldiers, many of them teenagers, going to battle, one had mixed emotions. Happy that the day had arrived when Hitler was going to get a taste of his own medicine, and sad knowing that so many of these boys were on a one-way ticket.

The departure of the Americans had left a void in my life and was the end of many happy months – an ending which had been so abrupt and final that I felt both sad and hurt that there had not even been a chance to say goodbye. The curfew a few days before they left had been unexpected. Extra guards were put around the base and, even with my intimate knowledge of the camp, there was just no way of getting in touch with my many friends. During the weeks that followed I did receive letters from a number of the boys, including the sergeant of 'K' but in most cases it was almost impossible to make any sense out of them as the letters arrived looking like a jig-saw puzzle which had not been completed with little rectangular holes where the censor had been at work. It was a month or so later that I heard from one of the boys that the sergeant had been killed in action somewhere in France.

I remember thinking, as a child, "He's dead and won't be returning home after the war and he had promised to invite me to visit him in America."

Now my dream to visit the land I had heard so much about would never come true.

I had promised myself after the Americans had left that I would never again visit the camp. What for? They had gone and there really was no point, but the temptation was too great. It had now been a number of weeks since their departure and I had decided on this Saturday morning that I would go and see for myself. Maybe they had not all gone – maybe just something remained – at least a reminder of the happy times I had spent there. As I approached the main gate along the dusty road, I could already see from a distance that the gate was wide open and as I entered the deserted compound, not a sound could be heard but the sound of chirping sparrows in the nearby bushes.

The wooden shutters and doors of each hut were firmly closed and nailed to every door was a notice that this was Government property, and it was forbidden to trespass. Turning the door handle very slowly, I found the door opened. Stepping inside I walked with care on the creaking floorboards, a little scared and not knowing what to expect. The only light was the light from the open door it was sufficient to show me what I had come to see. Here were the rows of familiar double bunks where I had spent so many hours of happiness, now deserted, damp and very silent. The only sound was the wind outside and the rustle of dried leaves, which were being blown through the door. All that was left of my world were dusty magazines in a heap in the corner and the odd screwed-up cigarette packet, which some G.I. had thrown on the floor. In the half-light the only sign of life that remained was the big-bosomed pin-ups looking down at me from the walls. They looked so silly with their voluptuous naked bottoms and provocative smiles. Leaving the door open I walked as if in a dream, a little dizzy and with a thousand confused thoughts running through my head. My visit confirmed, as I'd known, what I would find. There was no question about it – it was final, they had left. Never again did I return.

I felt even more restless and unhappy now and was even more of a nuisance to my foster parents and teachers.

The loss of my friends caused me to turn to my schoolmates for companionship. By now most of the boys had formed either close friendships with one or maybe two others, or else banded into gangs of boys with similar interests. I had not the drive nor the desire to force myself into an already cemented friendship so consequently found myself associating with the 'odd men out'. These, needless to say, were either those boys who had peculiar traits of character – often homosexual I think in retrospect – or else unbalanced temperamentally. One of these latter, a tall dark haired boy named Pete Granger had an uncontrollable temper. When roused he would bunch his fists up and lam out at all and sundry – even masters if they were the cause of his anger. He was always looking for ways to get his own back on the staff believing (probably correctly) that they enjoyed persecuting him. We had got into the habit of talking together at morning break while we drank our milk. The conversation usually took the form of discussion of the masters in the most derogatory way possible and one day he told me he needed my assistance to carry out a plan he had in mind.

"Have you ever been in the Staff room?" he asked me.

I shook my head. "No, but I've seen inside when I've been delivering messages."

"Well, I have and in the cupboard in the corner they keep their 'booze'. I want to get that cupboard open and sample some – that'll make them wonder!"

"But how are you going to do it?" I asked.

"You leave that to me. Stay behind after school tomorrow afternoon and I'll show you."

I didn't think it was a particularly good plan but I agreed to help him.

After the final bell the next day we carried out what was in fact the most difficult part of the whole operation. We had decided to hide in the cupboard under the stairs which was out of bounds because it housed the steps which led down to the cellar. We would of course, be locked in the school when everyone had gone but that was no problem because we had our own secret which was in and out of the school through the cloakroom window. It was difficult to get into the cupboard without being seen, but we managed it successfully and sat down on the top step to wait. The heavy door deadened the sound and we had to keep opening it slightly to see if the coast was clear. When we were sure we were alone we crept out and tip-toed along to the staff room.

Much to my admiration Pete had discovered where the spare key to the staff room was kept and had helped himself to it the day before.

Gingerly we inserted the key and turned it – the door opened. Carefully we lifted out two bottles, one of sherry and one of whisky. I tasted a little of each, but the whisky made me shudder – it was horrible. 'The sherry however, was sweet, and tasted quite pleasant.

I suppose we were there about an hour during which time I had consumed about half the bottle of sherry and Pete a little less from the other bottle. He looked terrible – I don't know how I looked but I felt most peculiar. My legs wouldn't support me and I felt so dizzy I could hardly stand!

I really don't remember how I got home – I can remember having to try several times to climb out of the window and also stumbling up the stairs when I got home but of the intervening time I have no recollection and as to at what stage Pete and I parted I had no idea. I was sick in the night but Mrs Carpenter made me go to school the next morning although I could not eat any breakfast. I had seen enough of the effects of alcohol in the American camp to know that I would feel ill but I'd never realised just how bad!

When I arrived at school I found the place buzzing with excitement. Pete Granger had been found at 7 a.m. lying on the staff room carpet, unconscious, smelling strongly of whisky and with a nearly empty bottle of the spirit clasped in his right hand. Nothing was said of my bottle of sherry and I certainly wasn't going to ask.

There was nothing to indicate that I had any part in the escapade and I did not see any point in owning up. Pete was taken to the sick bay and later transferred to the local hospital where he was treated for alcoholic poisoning. He never split on me for which I admired him greatly and was consequently expelled from school. I never saw him again – perhaps just as well for with his uncertain temper he might have decided I had failed him and there could easily have been two less boys in Form IIA.

In the next few weeks, convoy after convoy passed through the town on their way to ports in southern England. In most cases the boys were very young and unsophisticated, their helmets seeming to look far too big for them. Not knowing what was ahead for them but in anticipation that they would have to wade ashore on the other side of the Channel, someone had thought up the best way to protect their most valued possession - their bill-fold, containing family pictures of wives, children and sweethearts, which all soldiers carry. Contraceptives which were issued to men were ideal for this purpose. On a number of occasions I caught a young G.I. very embarrassed, trying to force a thick bill-fold into a rubber before tying a knot in it.

Most streets in town lined with horse-chestnut trees which provided natural camouflage from the air. Here the soldiers would stop to make final arrangements before being shipped across to France. The most important preparation they had to make was the water-proofing of their vehicles so that the engines would still be in good working order when driven ashore from the landing craft across the piers of the Mulberry Harbours to the shore of the French coast.

We watched with great interest the process they employed. They used a special sealer which looked like plasticine and which was so pliable it could be moulded very easily. It came in large drums and was packed around parts of the engine.

It wasn't until the final preparations had been completed that the men were told at last their exact destination. An order that only G.I. issued items were to be retained, and none of their personal possessions brought from the U. S. nor anything collected since being in England, presented a great problem to many of the soldiers.

Time was too short to allow any kind of organised sale of this quantity or stuff and most of it was just handed over indiscriminately to the townspeople who had been good to them – most of the householders had kept 'open house' during this time, the general policy being to 'adopt' the vehicle nearest to one's home, and provide what one could in the way of food and drink, the commodity most in demand being water for the weather was hot and the work dusty and tiring.

Piles of unwanted goods were often even left by the roadside for anyone to pick up and one day I found a pair of shoes made from expensive leather abandoned on the pavement. I thought how my farther would like them and picked them up. The trouble was that I did not know what size my father took in shoes, but nevertheless I took a chance and carried them carefully back home where I did them up in brown paper and posted them to London. In due course I received a 'thank you' letter from my father but I never found out if they were the correct size.

One night I was roaming round the town watching the soldiers work on their vehicles and rummaging through the piles of 'throw-outs' to see if there was anything else that might be of use to me or members of my family, when I felt a tap on my shoulder. I turned around and saw a swarthy-faced G. I. who had quite obviously been drinking.

"Wanna come with me? Got some candy back in m'room…" He lurched towards me and I smelt liquor on his breath. I should have had more sense but I nodded.

"C'mon," and taking me by the arm he began to lead me away from the main street and down a side road. Our progress was a little unsteady but it wasn't long before we reached one of the very second-rate hotels of the district. He beckoned me inside and up the stairs. There was a strong smell of stale cabbage water lingering in the air and the only light was from a single bulb suspended from the ceiling halfway up the stairs.

My heart began to thump and I began to regret my decision to accompany him. There was something about his manner apart from his drunkenness which was rather unsavoury. Once inside his bedroom he leaned heavily against the door and looked me up and down. Then he crossed to the bed on which there was an overnight bag and from it took a chocolate bar which he handed to me. He then produced a contraceptive from his trouser pocket and dangled it in front of my face.

"D'you know what this is for?"

Although I was not knowledgeable enough to know its exact use I knew it had something to do with sex because of the number of similar objects I had seen scattered around the perimeter of the camp.

"Yes," I whispered.

"You wait here – I'm just goin' to the John," and he went out of the room and down the corridor. Suddenly I knew instinctively that here was another man with the same liking for perversion as Private Symonds. I didn't know what was in store for me but I knew it would be unpleasant and without more ado I opened the door and ran down the stairs past the porters desk and out into the night. Passersby must have thought I was mad as I ran and ran until, exhausted, a mile or more away I had to halt, panting heavily and feeling wobbly at the knees. I was still clutching my chocolate bar which, with the heat from my hand, was now a sticky uneatable mess.

I learned later what my soldier friend had been expecting for his candy bar and looking back I do recall the fact that on the way to the hotel he had mentioned that he had recently been stationed in North Africa!

As the war progressed in France the types of troop convoy changed. From the early days directly after D-Day we had seen only infantry units pass through; now the beach heads had been secured in Normandy heavy artillery rumbled through the town daily, heading for the ports of embarkation. They were followed by heavy tanks. Monsters bigger than anything we had ever seen, soon passed through in their thousands becoming a daily sight, noisily crunching southward, cracking the pavements and leaving deep scars from their tracks on the roads. There was no let up. Soon soldiers of allied nations began to pass through as well. Belgian troops followed by Free French who were on their way home. One can imagine the eagerness of these boys after four years of enforced exile. The day had arrived when they could come face to face with those who had been responsible for the occupation of France and the cause of so much suffering to their families and country. The determination could be seen on their faces – they had the best reason in the world for fighting and they were ready and waiting, filled with bitterness and hate.

It was not only the language difference but their whole attitude particularly to us children that was so different from the G.I.'s. With our schoolboy French we tried to converse – it was the first time we had met anyone from France and the first time I had the opportunity to put my French to use. It was quite incredible that they understood even a few words, and they seemed flattered that we spoke to them in their own language and even more amazed that French was taught in English schools. They were so serious and much less fun than our American friends; they all seemed so preoccupied with their own thoughts they had little time for us. One of the most frightening sights was the arrival of the French Colonial troops, most of whom were as black as ebony – here was Africa in a small English market town. Many had pock-marked faces and to us they seemed very ugly and with their gleaming white teeth were the fiercest-looking humans we had ever seen. We were warned not to mix or talk with them and we hurried by them in the streets. After all we had heard about blacks, this seemed to confirm everything!

To make matters worse many of these barbaric-looking creatures sat around in the daytime sharpening with great nonchalance cruel-looking knives which they looked quite capable of using at the slightest provocation. During the few days they were in town many parents would not let their children out of the house unaccompanied, and I never saw one family offer them any kind of hospitality – so different from what they had shown to the visitors of previous months.

ITALIAN PRISONERS OF WAR

I am always deeply moved to think of our men fighting side by side in so many fierce battles…
Sir Winston Churchill in a cable to President Roosevelt.

I suppose that for most of the time I was evacuated I was too young to be able to follow any sequence of event in the progress of the war. I had experienced the blitz; I had seen the filmed reports of great battles on the cinema newsreels and I had, of course, heard my American friends discussing in great detail, the various campaigns, but it was not until I became friendly with some Italian P.O.W.'s during the latter part of 1944 that I had any understanding of the Italian Campaign.

After the conquest of North Africa the next logical step had been the invasion of Sicily. This was planned by General Alexander – Eisenhower's deputy – and under the direction of General Montgomery and divisions of the Eighth Army and General Patton with divisions of the Seventh Army, this was very successfully accomplished. On August 17, 1943, General Alexander sent a telegram to Winston Churchill stating:

"By ten a.m. this morning August 17th, 1943 the last German soldier was flung out of Sicily and the whole island is now in our hands."

Italy had been under the dictatorship of Mussolini for twenty-six years but growing unrest in the country resulted in his overthrow at this eventful time and the King was restored as overall monarch. This was a blow for Hitler because Mussolini had kept Italy as Germany's ally, but the King now signed an armistice with the British and American governments which added great zest to the invasion. The fascists, however, rushed to join the German forces – mainly in the north of the country – and although when the Allies invaded the 'toe' at Reggio they met little opposition and were able to press on northwards to Pizzo and Cantanzaro where it became a harder and harder slog through difficult country.

It was decided to land part of the Eighth Army at Salerno in order to hasten the advance whose eventual destination was Rome. It was a hard battle but the Allies were victorious and advanced to Naples, another port of great strategic importance.

The P.O.W.'s I have mentioned were only a few of the many thousands of Italians who had been either captured or, more likely, had surrendered during the North African campaign. Help was desperately needed on the farms where they were short-handed and those who wished, could work on the farms, which for many was a pleasant alternative to being locked up in a P.O.W. camp behind barbed wire for the duration of the war. Those who did volunteer were relatively free to wander around, unguarded but easily distinguished by their dark brown ex-army uniforms which had football-size yellow circles sewn onto their backs and their trousers. Never during the war did the English have any real hate for the Italians. Unlike the Germans where, through successful brainwashing, we all believed that "the only good Jerry was a dead one," we had a different and less violent attitude towards the Italians, particularly after the armistice.

The Government decided that they would not be a security risk, and for these handsome looking P.O.W.'s it was an easy life, and a pleasant one. They could be seen walking around the town, drinking beer in the local pubs after their day's work on the farm was done, and enjoying the pleasures of female company. It is impossible to know how many local girls, and even married women who had husbands away fighting, found the charms of these handsome Latin lovers too much to resist. Others had girlfriends whom they later married – liked the English way of life and never returned to their native Italy after the war.

My friends lived in a small cottage, some mile or so from my home. They had been given this tumbledown cottage to live in by the farmer, so they had little distance to travel to work each day. It had not been inhabited for years, but the thatched roof, with hundreds of holes in it where birds had nested, still kept out the rain. Situated in a meadow, it was a peaceful setting looking onto a clear stream, and at one time must have been lived in by a modest farmer or gamekeeper before it was abandoned. The interior had very little furniture, apart from two broken chairs and a table which they had made themselves from an old wooden crate. Most of the windows no longer had glass in them and were boarded up, for light they used an oil lamp which gave off a ghostlike glare, casting large soft shadows of the objects in the room.

After a number of visits the Italians and I became friends, spending long hours trying to converse with a mixture of my schoolboy Latin and French and their almost non-existent English. The use of our hands was invaluable and we would have understood much less without them. It was with them I hunted rabbits, using dogs and a spade. The dogs would follow the scent of a rabbit and lead us to its burrow where we would dig and dig until it was possible to reach the last few feet with an arm. Many times the work was for nothing but, on the other occasions, a rabbit would be dragged out of the hole by his feet or by his ears and within minutes would be skinned and on the roast. The meal of roast rabbit and vegetables stolen from the farmer would be prepared with herbs which they found in the countryside, producing sweet odours while the food cooked and having a taste which was quite new to me. Any rabbits shot but not required for the pot were sold for two shillings with three pence extra for the skin. It was a profitable business and my friends seemed to want for nothing, always seeming to have an ample supply of cigarettes, beer as well as a variety of foodstuffs – I think it must have been their charm as much as their money which accounted for this.

One of the most intriguing things I learned was how to make wine – something that until then I had never tasted. The most popular kind was made from elderberries which I helped them collect but they also brewed parsnip as well as dandelion wine.

First the berries had to be stripped from the stalks and put in a huge bath they had procured from somewhere. Then boiling water was poured over the berries and they were left until the next day. The contents of the bath were squeezed through a very thin cloth and the rich-looking liquid would then be boiled up with sugar, raisins, ginger and cloves and later yeast was added. Where the Italians managed to get enough sugar from I have no idea but the end product – after the wine had been left for about two weeks in cask – was the most delicious and potent stuff I had ever tasted. One of the Italians was a tall blond Milanese who one day asked me if I would take a photograph of him to send back to his family, for since the armistice, postal services to Italy had been resumed. I did as he wished and he was very grateful. The extraordinary sequel to this anecdote is that years later when I was grown up and in business I happened to be in Rome and found it necessary to hail a taxi. The traffic problem in Rome is one of the worst in Europe and during the journey we got talking and I was impressed by his command of the English language and I complimented him on it. "I was for several years in your country," he told me. "I was a prisoner of war in a little English market town."

I looked at him more closely and saw that he seemed remarkably familiar – it was my Milanese friend from the cottage. He was as delighted as I to renew our acquaintance and in fact we kept in touch by letter until he died ten years later.

After the comparatively easy early stages of the invasion of Italy the Allies met very strong resistance from the German forces. It looked as if Rome would be difficult to take. The supreme commanders decided to land troops at Anzio beach and two divisions – the 1st British Division and the 3rd U.S. Division – an attack was launched.

At roughly the same time an attack was made on the German stronghold at Monte Cassino which involved the 10th British Corps and the 2nd U.S. Corps well supported by the joint Air Forces. After much arguing as to whether the bombing of the monastery which adjoined the German garrison was ethical, this manoeuvre was carried out but the advancing troops were beaten back and Cassino did not fall.

At Anzio also the advance was not proceeding as well as hoped and eventually a section of troops was sealed off at the beach head by the German attack and the main army could not advance from the south. It was a dangerous situation and the enemy was in a strong position. Field Marshal von Kesselring prepared for a major attack to drive the British and Americans into the sea. In his book 'Closing the Ring', Winston Churchill says:

"The attack fell at an awkward moment, as the 45th U.S. and 56th British Divisions transferred from the Cassino front were just relieving our gallant 1st Division who soon found themselves in full action again. A deep, dangerous wedge was driven into our line, which was forced back here to the original beach head. The artillery fire, which had embarrassed all the occupants of the beach head since they landed reached a new intensity. All hung in

the balance. No further retreat was possible. Even a short advance would have given the enemy power to use not merely their long-range guns in harassing fire upon the landing stages and shipping but to put down a proper field artillery barrage upon all intakes or departures. I had no illusions about the issue. It was life or death. But fortune, hitherto baffling, rewarded the desperate valour of the British and American armies. Before Hitler's stipulated three days the German attack was stopped. Then their own salient was counter-attacked in flank and cut out under fire from all our artillery and bombardment by every aircraft we could fly. The fighting was intense, losses on both sides were heavy, but the deadly battle was won.

One more attempt was made by Hitler – for his was the will-power at work – at the end of February. The 3rd U.S. Division on the eastern flank was attacked by three German Divisions. These were weakened and shaken by their previous failure. The Americans held on stubbornly and the attack was broken in a day, when the Germans had suffered more than 2,500 casualties. On March 1st Kesselring accepted his failure. He had frustrated the Anzio expedition. He could not destroy it."

Eventually after re-grouping the forces in Italy to reinforce those already engaged at Anzio and Cassino, a major effort was made to destroy the enemy south of Rome in order to facilitate the entry and capture of the city.

Monte Cassino was taken after bitter fighting on May 18th, and the breakout from Anzio was accomplished on May 25th. From then on the march to Rome was in progress.

The P.O.W.'s had an ancient wireless set which someone had given them. My Milanese friend was something of an expert on radio and he had spent many hours fiddling with wires and valves and great was the day of triumph when, amidst much crackling of static he managed to tune in to the B.B.C. European Service broadcasting in Italian.

We followed the reports of the many battles and skirmishes leading up the taking of the capitol, and it was with mixed feelings that I heard – while in their company – that we had captured Rome on June 4th.

Occasionally we would listen in to the traitor William Joyce, broadcasting from Germany for the Nazis. Known as Lord Haw-Haw, he warned us of what the Germans had in store for us – and of the German divisions, barges and transport ships which were massing in preparation for the invasion to be. Lord Haw-Haw with his sneering manner of speech, who had prophesied the occupation and destruction of Britain, was hanged in London for treason, after the war on January 3, 1946.

I also developed a taste for Opera through listening with the Italians to the wireless, an appreciation I was glad to have later in my life.

I suppose I gained more from my friendship with these P.O.W.'s than anyone else with whom I came in contact. Because they had more free time than many people, including the G.I.'s, they always seemed willing to join me in the things I wanted to do. Apart from the rabbiting sessions and the wine making and tasting they accompanied me on many enjoyable cycle rides.

One Saturday my Milanese friend – whose name was Vicenzo – and I decided to go out for a whole day. We wanted to go as near to the coast as we could because we had heard there was an interesting stretch of completely straight beach formed by a shingle bank several miles long and that where the bank trapped the water large lagoons were formed.

We let off about 9 o'clock with packs of bread and margarine, apples and a bottle of elderberry wine in Vincenzo's saddlebag. It was a glorious day and the countryside looked green and lush in the summer sunshine. By now Vicenzo and I could communicate quite well – his English had improved considerably since he had begun to listen to broadcasts in English as well the Italian Service. We chattered as we pedalled along and he compared the scenery with that of his homeland.

At last, breasting a hill we saw before us the sparkling sea. Sure enough the deserted shingle beach stretched for mile upon mile. As we got nearer we could see a large stretch of water upon which were sailing literally hundreds of swans! I had never associated swans with the sea. In fact I had only seen them on isolated occasions – at the zoo, sometimes in London parks and once or twice when we had been to the river. The sight of so many graceful white birds floating amicably was breathtaking.

We learnt a little later as we chatted to the postman in the adjacent village that this was in fact a Swannery and had been in existence for hundreds of years. Before the war, apparently, people would travel miles to visit this famous place.

Another source of delight was the fact that the Italians were very fond of football. Whenever I wanted practice at this, my favourite game, I had only to take my ball up to the cottage and one or more of the P.O.W.'s would come out and start kicking it around. They became so keen that eventually they began to wish they could play a proper game. Now it so happened that there was another P.O.W. camp not far away and during the winter months the two groups of Italians met several times in one or two of the local public houses. It was suggested they should form a football team. Everyone was most enthusiastic. The next thing was to find some opposition to play against. I told the sports master at school about my friends and he agreed to allow the first eleven to play a friendly match. The day dawned bright and clear – the ground hard but playable. We turned out in force to watch this most unusual contest. It was very difficult for me. I knew I should cheer on my school but my support was really for the visitors.

It was quite a good game in spite of the fact that the Italians were playing with only nine men. At half time the score was five to four to the school. Then in the second half Vincenzo scored two magnificent goals to make the final score six – five to the P.O.W.'s.

After this success the Italians played several matches with teams from the nearby villages – very mixed teams they were too with most of the men called up for active service and the players' ages ranging from fifteen to sixty-five. I felt rather proud, however, that I had been the instigator of this very satisfactory arrangement. One of the P.O.W.'s from this other settlement had been a stonemason before being called up to join the Italian Army. He was a small olive-skinned black-eyed man who gave the impression of having immense energy waiting to burst forth. He could never lounge around in the tea-break like the others but always had to be doing something. They were engaged on building a road which would link two fairly busy roads into the town and one day having nothing better to do I cycled out to watch them. I was intrigued to see this man – I think his name was Guiseppi – chipping away at a block of the local stone from which the base of the road was being constructed. As I watched the form he was creating began to emerge – the head and shoulder of what appeared to be a Greek (or maybe Roman) god. He worked with an intensity and purposefulness that was new to me. After a while his mates called him to continue hewing the stone for the road and he turned to this with as much single-mindedness as to his sculpting.

I returned several times to the site and was amazed to find the road bordered by several of these magnificent statues. Maybe they are still there for Guiseppi certainly never could have had them removed!

Yes, all in all the Italians had quite a beneficial effect on my cultural education.

FLYING BOMBS AND V2 ROCKETS LAND ON LONDON

We have come safely through the worst!
Sir Winston Churchill.

In August 1944 I was allowed home once more. Looking back it seems strange that on both occasions I returned to my native city it was under air attack. The first time, of course, was during the blitz and this time, the latest German weapon the 'Doodle-Bugs' were being launched against London. These secret weapon attacks had begun after the Normandy landings and Hitler's campaign was now in full swing.

The Doodle-Bug was a radio controlled rocket and was so called by the Londoners because a few moments before it reached its target the motor would cut out and it would doodle or glide along silently before diving to earth and exploding. It was an unnerving experience to hear this droning noise suddenly stop and to look up and see one of the bugs which looked like small monoplanes – approaching in the sky. They were ejected from firing platforms stationed along the northern coast of France and came in vast numbers – as many as 100 or 150 a day. Considering they only weighed about one ton the damage they did on exploding was unbelievable – much of it the effect of blast. I was to see a horrible example of what these rockets could do after I had been in London only a few days.

A hostel for African students a block or so from the University had received a direct hit. The building itself which had been a classic Georgian house had been completely destroyed and was now utterly unrecognisable. The bodies of dozens of black students lay mixed in with the smouldering rubble. Some of the bodies were whole. There were also pieces of bodies blown hundreds of yards – hands, legs and heads – not looking as if they had ever been alive and had been part of a human being.

One of my worst recollections was on a Sunday morning when over one hundred and fifty of a congregation were killed outright, and many more died in hospital from their terrible injuries after the church had received a direct bit by a flying bomb; the sound of dozens of ambulances rushing towards the scene of what had been the church and the rescuers dragging bodies out, many who were dead from the rubble. Passersby were assisting the rescue work, including a number of American servicemen who had been nearby when the rocket had hit the church.

Following the V1 rocket attacks which we thought would be the last form of air attack we would have to endure in London, the Germans launched their final and even more destructive weapon on us. It was another pilotless missile - the V2 rocket. It had a more powerful warhead than the Doodle-Bug and caused greater damage. Achieving greater heights before descending and exploding it was neither possible to see nor hear its approach. During my stay I worked very hard on my father to try to persuade him to let me leave school at the end of the coming term. He was very disappointed at my lack of interest and progress at school. I had really only excelled myself on one occasion and that was when I had won the Divinity prize.

The Prize-giving was held in the local cinema and it was one of the major highlights of the school year (the others being Sports Day and the School Concert). On this occasion I had been told a few days previously that I had won a prize – I was so surprised I could hardly believe it – and I had to sit in one of the first three rows of the cinema to facilitate the continuity of the stream at boys mounting the steps to the platform. I had told my foster parents of my success thinking they might like to join the audience of parents, but they were not very interested or impressed and they did not come. When my turn came I mounted the steps with care and shaking the hand held out to me received my prize, a large and sombre looking book on the Scriptures.

It seemed a somewhat adult book for one of my tender years and as it was not a subject in which I had much interest anyway, on my return home I duly presented it to Mr Carpenter thinking it might please him enough to reduce the number of beatings lined up for me in the future. He took it without so much as a 'thank you'.

My father tried to countermand my reasons for leaving school with reasons of his own as to why I should stay on. His ambition was that I should eventually go to University which in the circumstances was very generous of him for the financial position of my parents was still extremely precarious. I was absolutely determined to leave school as soon as it was legally possible for me to do so and as my fourteenth birthday came after the end of the Christmas holidays I did not see much point in going back.

By the end of my stay in London – spent it seems in retrospect listening for the 'cut out' of Doodle-Bugs and diving for the nearest shelter – I had worn him down and I returned to the country for the last time.

In November 1944, Sir Winston Churchill, who had inspired us through those long hard war years, was to speak on the American Day of Thanksgiving in London. Now it so happened that this event coincided with half-term, and my father managed to obtain permission for me to return to London. The headmaster discouraged long-distance travelling for short periods but I suppose he thought the reason for my father's request a valid one. With a light heart I set off once more for the station – I was really becoming quite a seasoned traveller. It was a bright though cold morning and the countryside was very beautiful with the trees still carrying their leaves of yellow and brown.

When we had been going for about half an hour the train stopped suddenly for no apparent reason. We sat and waited. The adults in the carriage began to hazard guesses as to what was the matter, and one soldiers opened the window and leaned out. With the open window came the unmistakeable smell of burning.

"Oi 'opes as 'ow this 'ere train baint be on foire!" the speaker in this broadest of western dialects was a large buxom woman sitting in the corner. "Oi couldn't possibly jump from train to save me loif!"

"I don't think it is the train that's on fire," said the soldier bringing his head in from the window as a billow of smoke swirled by. "I think it's something on the line."

The smoke was much thicker now and small burning particles were blowing through the window. The soldier shut it quickly. The women in the carriage began to look anxious. The smoke became so dense it reminded me of that first journey down from London when the fog came down and blotted out the view.

Suddenly along the farm road which ran alongside the railway line came a roaring of engines and clanging of a bell – the local fire engine was coming to the rescue! This excitement was too much for the soldier who opened the door and jumped down onto the line. Heart in mouth I followed him. Most of the passengers had in fact descended on to the track and were hurrying to see what it was that was burning so fiercely. When the soldier and I reached the front of the train we saw that a large haystack in the field next to the railway was nearly burnt away. The top part of it had actually fallen on the track in front of the engine and now formed a black squelchy mess where the water from the hoses had saturated the hay.

Eventually the line was cleared enough to enable the train to proceed on its journey but we were now nearly three quarters of an hour late – I hoped my father would wait for me as I knew we hadn't a great deal of time to get to the Albert Hall where the meeting was to be held. The engine driver must have broken all records for the run as he pushed the engine along at breakneck speed. As we pulled into the Main Line station the clock read ten minutes past six – only fifteen minutes late. My father's anxious gaze relaxed as he saw me pushing through the crowds.

"You're late," he cried as I hugged him. The story of my adventure lasted all the way home!

The Hall was packed to capacity with people who had come to hear the man who was so loved and so admired by all English men and women, and to whom we owed so much.

He spoke of what this day of Thanksgiving meant to the American people, and went on to say that this peace-loving people of the United States had, through necessity in the short period of three or four years, become the greatest military, naval and air power in the world.

Sir Winston had continued:

"I have spoken of American Thanksgiving. Tonight, here representing vaster audiences and greater forces moving outside this hall, it is both British and American thanksgiving that we may celebrate. And why is that? It is because, under the compulsion of mysterious and all-powerful destiny, we are together. We are joined together, shedding our blood side by side, struggling for the same ideas, until the triumph of the great causes which we serve shall have been made manifest.

But there is a greater Thanksgiving day which still shines ahead, which beckons the bold and loyal and warm-hearted, and that is when this union of action which has been forced upon us by our common hatred of tyranny, which we have maintained during these dark and fearful years shall become a lasting union of sympathy and good feeling and loyalty and hope between all the British and American people, wherever they dwell. Then, indeed, there will be a Day of Thanksgiving, and one in which all the world will share."

It was a thrilling experience and one I shall remember all my life. During this last term at school I began to become conscious of stirrings of interest in girls. In spite of my rather sophisticated education in sexual matters during my association with the G.I.s, it had left me quite untouched physically.

On the way to school I had to pass a large red-brick building which was the local Girls' School. In the past this had been just an irritation – slowing down one's bicycle in order to thread one's way through a crowd or girls, milling about and chattering away in high-pitched voices was a bore in my younger days, but now I began to be fascinated by the varying shapes and sizes the female form could take.

On one unforgettable afternoon my growing self-confidence was rudely shattered. It was a Thursday which meant Cricket, and dressed in impeccable white from head to foot, a friend and I were cycling home, in high spirits – I suppose we'd had a good game with some action for a change. I remember we were dashing along at high speed waving our cricket bats in the air like sabres. We careered madly along swooping together then away again – there was no other traffic on the road – when suddenly as we approached the Girls' School the peddle of my friend's bike caught in the front wheel of mine. There was a horrible crunching of metal meeting metal and I was hurled unceremoniously over the handlebars. I picked myself up gingerly, conscious of shrieks of feminine merriment. Through the windows of the school I could see many of the inmates convulsed with hysterical laughter. My trousers were ripped across the seat, my cap was minus its badge and the palms of my hands were raw and bleeding and imbedded with gravel. It was with red face and heavy heart I picked up the tangled mass of my precious bicycle and made a slow and painful journey home.

Somehow the things that had got me down previously no longer seemed so bad. The knowledge that in a few weeks I would be leaving the vicinity forever gave me a fortitude that was very useful as with each day almost Mr Carpenter became more and more sadistic. The beatings I received from him became more and more frequent – and incidentally more and more painful. The cause was usually my disobedience to his commands. He always wore a pair of brown corduroy trousers, very worn and baggy which were supported by a pair of braces and a belt. This belt was of strong dark leather and had a brass buckle and his favourite form of punishment was to whip me across the bottom with it.

I remember one particular occasion when I had boxed John's ears for telling tales on me, my foster father was furious. He lashed out at me so hard that he knocked me to the ground. Not only was all the breath knocked out of my body but my precious pocket watch, my prized possession given to me by my father, fell from my pocket on to the hard floor. Grabbing it and holding it to my body I shouted: "If you've broken it, I'll…" but not trusting myself to finish the sentence I rushed to my room sobbing – I think it was the only time he managed to reduce me to tears. My watch was mercifully intact and I have it to this day, it's engraved inscription: "To David, 9th Birthday. Love Daddy," almost indecipherable through constant wear.

Another example of Mr Carpenter's malicious nature can be seen in the matter of my stamp collection. Philately is another somewhat solitary hobby like birds' eggs collecting, and this, I suppose, is why it appealed to me. Over the years I spent with my foster parents I managed to build up quite a sizable collection of which I was rather proud. I had been forbidden by Mr Carpenter to take the Album to school but one day having just acquired a magnificent specimen whose design was a Bird of Paradise, I succumbed to temptation.

"After all," I argued to myself, "what's the use of having something special if you can't show it off?"

So I took it to school where it was duly admired. A few days later wishing to gloat over my latest possession I turned to the page where I had affixed the Bird of Paradise – it had gone!

Although I usually kept my troubles to myself I was so upset by my discovery that I rushed downstairs where Mr and Mrs Carpenter were sitting, crying:

"My best stamp's gone!"

A sly smile spread across my foster father's face. Serves you right for taking it to school – I told you not to."

I said no more.

About a week later I was browsing through Mr Carpenter's 'nude magazines in his room when on opening one of the drawers of his desk I saw a familiar object. There laid on the front cover of a paper book was my Bird of Paradise. My foster father had presumably taken it to pay me back for disobeying his wishes. I crept to my room stunned by such cruel behaviour. Finally I fell asleep none the wiser as to the twisted sort of thinking that must have gone into this action.

I thought it a strange coincidence that our next door neighbour, Mr Johnson, was of a similar nature to my foster father. He was a really miserable-looking man who rarely spoke and it seemed to me that he had chosen a particularly appropriate profession to fit his appearance – that of a warder at the nearby prison. He would cycle to work every day – not always at the same time because he worked on a shift – dressed in his drab prison uniform. Black cap with H.M..P. on the badge and a long black coat which always seemed in imminent danger of catching in the wheels but somehow never did! From the back he looked like a giant bird of prey as he hunched over the handlebars pedalling laboriously along the road. His wife, in direct contrast to him, was a tall, cheerful, ruddy-faced woman. She never wore any make-up and her red rosy cheeks looked as if they had been scrubbed with soap and water –

which maybe they had, as in common with Mrs Carpenter she kept her family and house spotlessly clean.

As the families seemed to be so alike it intrigued me why they never associated with one another. The two women would politely pass the time of day if they came face to face in the street or when they both appeared in their gardens together to hang out the Monday morning's wash, but that was the sum total of their socialising. They had two boys whom we did not see very much as they were not really in the same age groups as either John or myself and who anyway, went to different schools, but I noticed that any contact there was, was definitely discouraged. Eventually I discovered why. They were catholic and so 'different from us'. Mr Carpenter would refer darkly to our Catholic neighbours if ever he had to mention them – never by name.

As I got older and more independent I disregarded Mrs Carpenter's wishes and went out of my way to speak to the boys and in fact during the last summer we found ourselves working side by side on a farm in the holidays. One day I asked Tom, who was the nearest to me in age, what being a Catholic was like.

"T'is no different from being anyone else Oi reckon," he said after a pause. "We go to church more'n what you do – never miss a Sunday, we don't and Mass midweek as well sometimes."

"Who says you got to go so much?"

"Well, Pope, I s'pose – he's Head of the Church."

"Is he a God?" I asked, puzzled by this mysterious person.

"God do speak thru' him," Tom answered gravely.

"What do you do in church that's different?"

"Oi dunno, Oi never bin ter yer church – we says prayers and sings hymns then we go to Confession."

"Confession?"

"Aye – we go tell t'priest what naughty things we done."

"Do you <u>have</u> to?"

"Oh aye."

"How awful!"

"No t'aint – t'is good – we don't feel so bad about what we done when we've confessed."

"Do you get punished?"

Tom nodded.

"What sort of punishment?"

"Well, sometimes we has to say extra 'Hail Mary's' and sometimes we has to promise not to do the bad things again."

"Do you <u>have</u> to tell the truth?"

"Oh yes."

"What sort of bad things do you have to tell about?"

Tom thought for several minutes.

"Well, last Sunday he asked me: 'Do you love God? Do you always come to Mass on Sundays? Do you tell lies?' This was all to do with the Ten Commandments, see?"

I thought what an intelligent boy Tom must be to be able to carry on a conversation like this with a priest.

He continued: "Then he asked me: 'Do you do dirty things?' and of course I had to say: 'Yes'."

Then Tom repeated to me the words of Father Timothy which were to have a lasting effect on me for a number of years.

"Children who play with their private parts, apart from being sinful, make themselves consumptive and DIE!"

I was silent for a minute.

"What's consumptive?"

"It's a terrible disease you get when your lungs all go bad and you can't breathe."

I was terrified. If this was true half the boys at school would be dropping dead any minute and I wasn't sure I didn't qualify for this untimely death as well. At this moment my interesting talk with Tom was interrupted and I don't think we ever got down to such a serious discussion again.

From our school building we could see the massive prison that I mentioned earlier in connection with Mr Johnson. The windows were of course, all barred, and sometimes we would see arms hanging between the bars as the inhabitants of the cells, obviously hearing our shouts and laughter, tried to form some contact with the living world outside. Sometimes we could see something white and presumed it was a handkerchief or a piece of paper that some poor unfortunate inmate was using to try to attract our attention. Sometimes we would use a piece of broken glass to reflect the sun's rays and would flash it into the cells – we were often rewarded by the sight of an arm waving pathetically back to us. I vowed to myself that it I were shut up inside such a dreadful place I wouldn't hesitate – I'd escape.

Someone obviously shared my feelings on the subject because one day there was a breakout from the prison. There was great excitement in the school of course. We were so near that our premises and grounds were always the first to be searched on these occasions. All the pupils were mustered in the Hall where the headmaster called the roll to make sure everyone was present. Then the police and the prison warders searched everywhere a prisoner might hide – always apparently to no avail for there was no history of any prisoner ever being caught at the school.

This time there was extra excitement because a rumour quickly spread that the prisoner who had escaped was of a violent nature and had in fact, severely injured one of the warders. Of course he was nowhere to be seen and much to our disappointment lessons were very soon resumed. He was, I believe, caught several months later trying to leave the country but we never really learnt the true story.

An interesting corollary however, was the fact that Mr Johnson died only a few days after the breakout. Mrs Carpenter told me that our neighbour had died as a result of injuries sustained from falling out of an apple tree. I found this very strange. Whoever heard of anyone dying through falling out of a tree? I suppose if one fell from a great height and broke one's neck this was quite possible but the Johnson's had no tree higher than about five feet. I asked many questions and really got no satisfactory answers and I am convinced to this day that Mr Johnson was the victim of an attack by the prisoner who had escaped. I never found out the truth.

Mrs Carpenter told me that we were going to go to 'their' church to 'pay our respects'. I was quite excited that at last I was going to get some idea of the mysteries that went on at a Roman Catholic service.

As the day approached for us to go to the funeral I noticed that Mrs Carpenter was becoming edgy and nervous. She would not tell me how it might differ from our own church and when I asked her what I should do she replied sharply: "Just be still and do what the rest of the congregation do."

It was a grey day and dressed in our best Sunday clothes we all set off for the funeral. The church was at the other end of the town and it took us quite a time to walk there – Mrs Carpenter kept fussing that our shoes were getting dusty and that it wasn't fitting that we should arrive looking shabby.

Inside, the church had a foreign feel about it. I think it was probably the smell of the incense which I had never experienced before and the sombre chanting in Latin – of which I understood nothing, although we were being taught Latin at school.

The priest was dressed in robes of deep rich colours – he looked almost theatrical, and as he intoned the words of the service, the sun came out and shone through the stained glass windows making a pattern like a Kaleidoscope on the stone floor in front of him. The affect of all this colour was breathtaking and I felt more religious than I had ever done in church before.

It was a long service and every so often a little bell would ring. I longed to ask what it meant but the heads around me were bent in reverence and even John seemed awed by it all.

At last the service was over and solemnly we all filed out in the wake of the pall-bearers to the graveyard at the back of the church. Here I saw for the first time the deep hole where the remains of Mr Johnson were to be laid to rest. The wind was cold and everything seemed still and dead. The trees were dropping their leaves and a few, twisted and brown fluttered into the open grave. As the coffin was lowered the priest said some more prayers and sprinkled what I learnt afterwards was holy water from a container that looked exactly like the sugar sprinkler we had at home. Then it was over. Back home, we joined the mourners in the little front room in the next door house to offer condolences for the loss of Mr Johnson. I stood back and listened to the conversations going on around me.

"How good he was…"

"What a fine father your husband was, Mrs Johnson…"

"A great loss to the community…"

"He did a fine job…"

Could all these people really be speaking of that miserable and bigoted man who lived so near for so long and never spoke a kindly word to us and who used to beat his children even more regularly than Mr Carpenter beat me?

How strange was human nature to be so conditioned by circumstance that their honesty should be so impaired!

Finally Home – World War II Is Over

God bless them all. This is your victory!
Sir Winston Churchill, 1945.

Nineteen-forty-five and home at last. The war not over but the Allies were well on the way to victory.

Immediately the Christmas holiday was over I started looking for a job and within a few days of searching the newspapers 'Situations Vacant' column I found an advertisement for a boy to work in a photographic shop helping to pack parcels, run errands and make the tea.

Putting on my best school trousers and a jacket of my father's I presented myself for an interview. The shop was in a rather unsavoury back street and was dingy and depressing but they appeared to do quite a good trade, because while I was being interviewed in the back room the bell in the shop rang several times.

I felt jubilant when after questioning me quite closely on what I thought a strange variety of subjects, the man, whose name, I think, was Mr Masters said I could have the job. I was to report for work the following Monday morning at 9 o'clock and my wages would be thirty shillings a week out of which I would have to pay my own Income Tax.

I shall never forget my first job. The windows of the shop were protected by two massive rusty iron gates to prevent anyone smashing the windows during the night and making off with the rather meagre selection of photographic equipment on display. These gates were ludicrous as they looked more suitable for protecting the Crown Jewels than the few cameras and tripods, and the amount of effort involved in removing them in the morning and replacing them at night seemed out of all proportion. This, needless to say, was my responsibility.

I had to carry these gates down a winding staircase into the basement, which wasn't too bad until I discovered on my second morning that the place was over-run with rats. It was very dark – in fact the dark-room itself was at the far end - and one could see an occasional red eye gleaming in the far corner and hear the scampering as they disappeared down the large oval-shaped holes in the skirting-board. I was scared and began to hate going down~ there. I would whistle and stamp my feet and make as much noise as possible in order to frighten them away before I got down there. My second job of the morning was to sweep the entire entrance and the pavement outside the door of the shop. Street sweepers were few and far between during the war because of the shortage of labour but people were just as untidy and the amount of litter that accumulated was amazing.

I was not allowed to serve in the shop – in fact I was not allowed to even touch any of the camera equipment and after the novelty of having a job of my own began to wear off I began to puzzle out how I could really learn something constructive about my chosen trade. Suddenly I had an idea. Every evening on my way home I was supposed to take the parcels I had done up during the day, to the Post Office.

I started taking them home with me instead. They were either pieces of new equipment going to customers or else old parts going to be repaired. Carefully I would undo all my neat parcels and lay the contents out on the top of my chest of drawers – cleared for this purpose. I was very careful to keep note of what came out of which parcel. For several evenings I would study the cameras and photographic equipment, memorising the different pieces and their functions, then I would meticulously re-do the parcels and take them to the Post Office on my way to work the next morning.

Next door to the shop was a Snooker Hall and it soon became my habit to spend my lunch hours in here. At first I would just watch the games as I chewed my way through cheese and chutney sandwiches, then one day, having at last saved up enough money I 'had a go' myself and found it fascinating. From then on I played whenever I could and eventually became quite proficient.

About three months after I had first started to play, a man whom I'd never seen before entered the Hall. He was dark and very thin-faced and he was very well dressed. He spoke well and seemed a very respectable type, and came over to where I was practising. "Play you a game - winner buys lunch?" he asked without preamble. It so happened that I'd had no lunch and I was very hungry and it seemed a good idea, so I nodded. We played and to my surprise I won! He gave me half-a-crown.

"Well done – you're a good player. Go and buy yourself some sandwiches." I went off well pleased with myself.

A couple of days later he came again.

"Have another game?"

I agreed.

"Play you for a quid?"

I felt my heart beat with excitement – I was sure I could win again. How innocent I was! I soon learned that this 'modus vivendi' of the 'Billiard Hall Lizards' was a well-known technique. They would find enough 'suckers' or 'Greeners' like myself and after playing a game or two and losing purposely would suggest a game for higher stakes and proceed to win. In this way they could keep themselves quite comfortably without much effort.

During this time dramatic things were happening in Europe and America. President Roosevelt died suddenly on April 12. His death was a terrible shock and a tragic loss to the world. He was mourned universally and many tributes were paid to him, among them from the Japanese Premier:

(President Roosevelt) "was responsible for the Americans' advantageous position today."

The German Western Front collapsed and Eisenhower crossed the Rhine. The Russians were only thirty-five miles east of Berlin. The end of April brought victory of General Alexander's campaign in Italy which surrendered unconditionally on the 29th, and on the same day Hitler at his H.Q. in Berlin – now surrounded by the Russians – made his will. The next day a shot was heard from his private room in the bunker– Hitler had committed suicide.

The next day the Russians entered the capital and chaos reigned. The instrument of total unconditional surrender was signed by Lieutenant General Bedall-Smith and General Jodl with French and Russian officers as witnesses at 2.41 a.m. on May 7. Thereby all hostilities ceased at midnight on May 8. The formal ratification by the German High Command took place in Berlin under Russian arrangements in the early hours of May 9. Air Chief Marshall Tedder signed on behalf of Eisenhower, Marshal Zhukov for the Russians and Field Marshal Keitel for Germany.

London went wild! There was dancing in the streets and not many people went to bed all night.

I went out with my parents but we soon got separated. I didn't mind. I was in my beloved London which I knew like the back of my hand - I was not likely to get lost. I made my way gradually to Piccadilly Circus, the hub of London's celebrations. It was while I was listening to people singing outside a public house to the accompaniment of a piano accordion that I found I was standing next to a girl of about my own age. She was of slight build and had blonde hair. She seemed to be alone but was quite unconcernedly humming to the music and clapping her hands. She noticed me looking at her and smiled. From that moment I was lost.

We spent the rest of the night wandering through the streets joining in the dancing when we felt like it and talking as if we'd known each other all our lives. To me it was a revelation. I had never known anyone I could really talk to. Although I had had many long sessions with the G.I.'s and the Italians, they had been somewhat one-sided with me doing most of the listening.

When we finally said goodbye it was with arrangements to meet again. That was how I met Sally and life took on a new dimension. When I wasn't out with Sally I spent my evenings locked in the lavatory at home, much to the inconvenience of my parents. This was because I had fitted it up as a dark-room in order to do some 'overtime'. There was a great shortage of all film including 35mm in cassettes and my employer paid me three pence for re-loading each cassette. I had acquired soma ex-Government Nitrate Base (highly inflammable) reels, each of 1,000 feet which I would cut into length of 5ft 3ins. – the equivalent of thirty-six exposures – to recharge each cassette. I reckon the shop made a good profit out of me for they resold them at one shilling and nine pence each, but I enjoyed the work and the money was useful. I'm sure the film must have got very scratched in my make-shift factory but no one ever complained as far as I know and I could earn between ten shillings and fifteen shillings per night by working non-stop for three hours. I was not allowed to commandeer the only toilet facilities in the flat for very long however and had to transfer my workshop to a large cupboard on the landing. This was completely unventilated and by half-way through the evening simulated a Turkish bath. I would strip down to my underpants while I worked but I still emerged dripping wet with perspiration at the end of the evening.

Unbeknown to the majority of the population, American scientists had been engaged on the manufacture of a new weapon which would end the war once and for all - the Atomic bomb.

Mr Churchill says in his book 'Triumph and Tragedy':

"I tell the tale as I recall it. The bomb, or its equivalent, had been detonated at the top of a pylon 100 ft high. Everyone had been cleared away for ten miles around and the scientists and their staffs crouched behind massive concrete shields and shelters at about that distance. The blast had been terrific. An enormous column of flame and smoke shot up to the fringe of the atmosphere of our poor earth. Devastation within a one-mile circle was absolute. Here then was a speedy end to the Second World War, and perhaps too much else besides...

To avert a vast indefinite butchery, to bring the war to an end, to give peace to the world, to lay healing hands upon its tortured peoples by a manifestation of overwhelming power at the cost of a few explosions seemed, after all our toils and perils a miracle of deliverance."

Two bombs were dropped on Japan within four days of each other. One on Hiroshima on August 6, and the other on Nagasaki on August 9. Japan finally surrendered on August 14, and the news was broadcast to the British people at midnight.

Once again there was joy and merry-making in the streets of London and once again Sally and I danced and sang with thousands of rejoicing people.

The war was over! And looking back I realize – so was my boyhood.

David L. Gordon

APPENDIX

Evacuation from London.

On September 1, 1939 I was to be sent away from London with a group of children between the ages of four and fourteen who were to be evacuated from London. We were loaded into cramped carriages at London's Waterloo railway Station. I was eight years old and my little brother John was four. Our unknown and mystery destination was to be Dorchester, Dorset, a country town of approximately 10'000 inhabitants. This safe haven in the country ironically suffered 784 air attacks by the German Luftwaffe during WW II with loss of life and 245 houses damaged by high explosive or incendiary bombs. Dorchester was a target for the German planes as there was a large military camp for British and later American troops. Also, in the near vicinity was the Royal Air Force base of Warmwell.

I was to learn later that some four hundred children had disembarked at Dorchester, the remaining children on the train were taken to other destinations.

Foster Parents.

In the school hall where the four hundred exhausted and bewildered children were gathered volunteer foster parents selected children like cattle. Many were doing it out of goodness of their hearts, while others saw an opportunity for financial gain.

The government was to pay 10 shillings and six pence per child per week for their upkeep.

Foster parents were advised that they must not 'swap' with other children billeted elsewhere. 'Swopping' was an offence.

Traumatised Evacuees.

They were from all classes of families, some of them from poor working class families. There were very real problems of hygiene, or lack of it, lice, and general cleanliness. Bed wetting was common by many of these scared, unloved and traumatised children in strange surroundings. Many were terribly beaten by their new foster parents.

Better Foster Parents – and a Better School

After our terrible experience with our initial foster home, John and I were saved by the child welfare authorities and transferred to a cleaner and nicer home where Mr & Mrs Carpenter, a childless couple, looked after our lives in a cold and unloving manner. How our lives had changed.

Before leaving London in the Summer of 1939, I had been, I can only presume, an outstanding student, and was awarded a London Junior County Scholarship which would entitle me to go to a Private School. The expensive school fees would be paid by the authorities. On arriving in Dorchester, I attended the normal school. We studied in shifts as with the influx of the London evacuees it was the only way the school could handle the newcomers. As luck would have it a teacher who had travelled with us from London took up my case and after much consultation with the local education authorities they agreed to honour my scholarship at the local Grammar school. Normally, they would only take students who could pay the hefty fees. I do remember her name was Miss West, that she was very ugly with a pock-marked face and on one occasion slapped my face for blotting my exercise book. Nevertheless, in retrospect, I am extremely grateful for all her efforts on my behalf.

A New School – Dorchester Grammar School.
Having been kitted out with my school uniform I started at my new school in early 1940. I still don't know who paid for my clothes which included cricket whites, cap, blazer and special socks. Maybe it was my foster parents or the local authorities - certainly not my parents who were in London and extremely poor at the time. The school was very snobby and a complete new experience for me. It was founded in 1618, and named the Thomas Hardy Freeschool, after its founder the famous writer Thomas Hardy. Later, in 1790 it was re-named Dorchester Grammar School. During my years at DGS my early thirst for knowledge which had won me a scholarship, did not continue and I became a very mediocre student preferring my own company and becoming somewhat introverted.

Looking back, no doubt I was missing my parents, their love and encouragement which I was certainly not getting in my present home. Rather than study I preferred to look out of the class-room window where I could count the aircraft taking off and landing at nearby Warmwell airstrip and imagining what it would be like to be a fighter pilot. Dogfights over Dorchester became a daily occurrence. We became experts at recognizing the Junkers, and the Stukas which made a terrifying screech as they dive bombed.

U.S. Troops arrive in Dorchester.
The first soldiers arrived in 1944, taking up quarters in Poundbury Camp. Many local girls were swept off their feet by these gum chewing, cigar smoking G.I.'s – resented by many of the locals, but not their generosity. Gifts of candy, cigarettes, chocolate and chewing gum were greatly appreciated in these wartime days of rationing. The most terrible fights took place between U.S. and other servicemen stationed in the area out of pure jealousy. Told they were 'overpaid, over-sexed and over here', their reply was you are underpaid, under-sexed and under Eisenhower. The American army was segregated in those days, so it was not until later that we saw black G.I.'s passing through the town on their way to France. Stories we heard from some of the racist white soldiers of how terrible the blacks were back home. For a young boy my acquaintance with our friends from across the Atlantic was quite an education.

Wartime rationing. (per person – weekly)
4 oz butter, 4 oz meat (when not available the alternative was Spam or Corned beef)
2 oz tea, 8 oz sugar, 4 oz jam, and 1 egg. 4 oz cheese

Citizens were issued with clothing coupons and even soap was rationed at 3 oz weekly.

People fared better in the country areas where vegetables and some fruit was plentiful.

Everyone was 'digging for victory' with every patch of land being cultivated. It is a fact that the nation had never been as healthy as it was during the war years.

D-Day June 6th 1944 and my friends leave for Omaha beach.

As mentioned earlier in my book, this day saw the departure of the U.S. 1st Infantry Division, called the big red one, and the many G.I. friends I had made. One especially I missed and can only remember – a tall handsome American called Sgt Cunningham. He was my friend, protector and the person who got me out of trouble when I was caught crawling under the barbed-wire to bring a quantity of fish and chips to his boys who were confined to barracks. I still have a scar on my upper leg from the razor-sharp barbed-wire. I wonder if he survived or if he was killed by a German bullet on Omaha beach?

After D-Day, convoys rolled through the streets of the town daily – tanks, guns, half tracks and lorries. The Sherman tanks ripping up the roads and pavements as they clumsily manoeuvred the corners of the narrow streets; briefly stopping to waterproof their vehicles and to dump any non issue equipment such as musical instruments, gloves, shoes or personal items which they may have accumulated. During this period I witnessed the soldiers squeezing bill folds containing pictures of their dear ones into condoms. These 'French letters' were also stretched over the top of their rifles as protection against sea water, knowing no doubt that they would soon be heading for the invasion beaches of Normandy. As a young boy I had never seen a condom before nor knew what their purpose was – so much for the sex education of the day. Taking one of these home and presenting it to Mrs Carpenter, my foster mother, I still did not find what they were used for, as red-faced she snatched it away from me adding 'this is nothing for you my boy'.

www.ingramcontent.com/pod-product-compliance
Ingram Content Group UK Ltd.
Pitfield, Milton Keynes, MK11 3LW, UK
UKHW041451180426
11946UKWH00013B/148/J